A New Age Child Is Born by Carol Ann Rodriguez

ON EARTH ASSIGNMENT

The Cosmic Awakening Of Light Workers, Walk-Ins & All Star-Born Representatives

ONLY AUTHORIZED EDITION

Inner Light Publications

ON EARTH ASSIGNMENT
The Cosmic Awakening Of Light Workers, Walk-Ins And All Star-Born Representatives

Original copyright held by Guardian Action Publications
Title transferred and new material added and copyrighted
© 1994/ 2014 Inner Light Publications

All rights reserved. No part of these manuscripts may be copied or reproduced by any mechanical or digital methods and no exerpts or quotes may be used in any other book or manuscript without permission in writing by the Publisher, Global Communications/Conspiracy Journal, except by a reviewer who may quote brief passages in a review.

Only Authorized Edition

Published in the United States of America By
Global Communications/Conspiracy Journal
Box 753 · New Brunswick, NJ 08903

Staff Members
Timothy G. Beckley, Publisher
Carol Ann Rodriguez, Assistant to the Publisher
Sean Casteel, General Associate Editor
Tim R. Swartz, Graphics and Editorial Consultant
William Kern, Editorial and Art Consultant

Sign Up On The Web For Our Free Weekly Newsletter
and Mail Order Version of Conspiracy Journal
and Bizarre Bazaar
www.ConspiracyJournal.com

Order Hot Line: 1-732-602-3407
PayPal: MrUFO8@hotmail.com

CONTENTS

TUELLA-A TRIBUTE by Brenda Payne iv

DEDICATION v

PREFACE vii

FOREWORD-VOLUNTARY EMBODIMENT by Lord Kuthumi ix

INTRODUCTION by Timothy Green Beckley xiii

Chapter One-Life's Highest Loyalty—MISSIONARIES FROM SPACE 1

Chapter Two-Life's Highest Commitment—COUNCIL OF COSMIC CAUSATION ... 29

Chapter Three-Life's Highest Purpose—SURRENDER 55

Chapter Four-Life's Highest Equipment THE CYCLES OF LIFE 75

Chapter Five-Life's Highest Lessons—PLANETARY LESSONS 95

Chapter Six-Life's Highest Comfort—NO SECOND CAUSES 119

Chapter Seven-Life's Highest Reward—THE MAGNITUDE OF THE MISSION 137

About Tuella 156

Tuella-A Tribute

A sculptor molds the lifeless clay
And creates works of art;
The singers sing impassioned notes,
And music from their golden throats
Can mold the human heart.
The chef prepares from nature's stores
And bids his fellows dine;
The counselor, with list'ning ears,
Helps ease one's pain and dry one's tears
To once more, souls align.
Physicians heal the house of flesh
And vibrant health restore;
And loving friends - one here, one there
By showing us that others care,
Lay gladness at one's door.
A teacher shapes the minds of those
Entrusted to his care;
With skill and patience, one who's wise
Can gently open others' eyes
While shielding them from glare.

"What is LOVE?" (We all have asked).
Those mentioned hold the key:

To do the task which lies at hand
In harmony, throughout the land
That each soul might just BE.
A shining spirit walks with us
From out the realms of love;
This one, with messages of Light,
Restores the blinded ones to sight,
Inspired by Those Above.
God sends such ones from time to time
From His celestial spheres;
To serve their fellows on this earth
Transfiguring from "death" to "BIRTH"
All those equipped with "ears."
We thank you, Lord, for such as she...
Who spread the LIGHT, that ALL might see.
-Brenda Payne

Dedication

This book is dedicated to all of God's Eagles wherever they may be upon the pathway back to the stars.

It is sent forth specifically for their edification.

As we focus attention upon the sameness of our spiritual adventures, we reinforce the majestic truth that we are one!

"Ashtar" as originally envisioned.

Preface

All of earth's volunteers have exalted moments they treasure from the secret places of the Most High. These pearls of great price are too personally profound and holy to share with another. These sacred moments often stun the devotee. They are left with mixed impulses, torn between hiding these revelatory times deep within the heart, or conversely, shouting them from the housetops.

These very personal encounters with the record of the soul provide us with vital self confidence and strength that will be needed later in the mission. We realize they are for us alone, too sacred to be shared.

I was no different than you. It has not been my policy to speak of the soul records of Tuella and her other manifestations on this and other planets. But now as I prepare for the return to the octaves of Home, I am guided to 'Share my glories with you. The reasons are threefold:

A. There is an aura of unbelief surrounding these early revelations. We tend to wonder about ourselves or think we are "out to lunch" mentally, or becoming fanatical. We doubt, we question, we reject. Perhaps as we see how it has been with others, we will recognize our own experiences.

B. All that you are, from whence you came, and why you are here will ultimately be pulled through your human consciousness in this embodiment, if you so desire. Much of this is necessary to the successful completion of your assignment. Thus the answers are there in your inner citadel. As a dedicated program of meditation is set into motion, these details will filter through the "voice of the silence." Keep a written record of these times and gradually the pure grains of truth will separate from the chaff of irrelevancies, and you, the human counterpart, will know that you know, that you know.

C. We are a Great Company. We are encompassed about by a great cloud of witnesses. It brings a warm glow to the soul to see in the experiences of others, the hallmark of Divinity we have within ourselves. A phrase of the world comes to mind, "It takes one to know one." It is comforting to know you are not alone in the humanness of it all.

- Tuella

Foreword

Voluntary Embodiment

by Lord Kuthumi

"In the Master's program for the enlightenment of Terra, down through many ages and eons and various cultures, there has always been the presence of those certain individuals whose work it was to experience a direct soul contact on telepathic levels with Universal Mind. In that way it was proposed that messages be relay6d to humanity for their help and guidance. Those certain ones have been called by many names: seers, prophets, patriarchs, mediums, channels, messengers and voices, oracles, and so on. It does not matter what terminology has been used by whatever culture or civilization, that instrument of God,, the mission, and often even the message, were always one. One individual chosen for that intercession would stand between the heavenly tribunals on behalf of existing humanity and be the receiver and sender of messages between heaven and earth.

"This was not a difficult thing for these instruments, because they, themselves, were serving the planet in a voluntary embodiment to serve the Brotherhood of Light in that capacity.

"In your day, you speak of earth-based Commanders. As impressive as that title may appear, it is nevertheless nothing new under the Sun. For your planet has had earth-based spiritual patriarchs since its earliest inception. These oracles, down through the corridors of time, have been,,in simpler terms, but messengers of the Gods. Behind every great religion that has touched the planet with challenge and depth, one finds these volunteering earth-based members of the inner Hierarchy serving quietly, deliberately, and often unknown until after their transition. We could progress, listing them all, from the ancient times down through many ages. The celestial government has never been without human representation upon the planet! Every new movement or revelation developing into a program of teaching and evolution has always been spawned from the heart of one individual soul, totally and completely God-centered in motive and purpose.

"As Light expanded upon earth, there were often many serving in such a capacity simultaneously, even beginning new movements which eventually became great world religions. It was those who followed after them who lost the message of Love, the vision of unity, and fostered earth destroying emphasis upon divisions. Return to the original creed of the earth's great spiritual pioneers, and one will always find Love at its core. For all of these founders were Hierarchical embodiments, appearing repeatedly to hold mankind in a spiritual quest upon the upward spiral.

"Because of certain times and lack of evolvement in many areas of man's history, the message was necessarily limited in kope to accommodate limited understanding. Light has been progressive, and it has **ALWAYS BEEN PRESENT**. It has sometimes appeared to be reduced to a flicker, but at every point in time of human history, Truth has always been cradled by an individual, a group or a country, appointed to be the guardian of truth for that time.

"Now that day has come upon the planet when there is to be a great flood of Hierarchical representation upon earth, externalizing its precepts and teachings for the masses. Because of much Light having been shed abroad in the land, now in this day of World Teachers, both incarnate and discarnates, can freely expound without limitations, the deepest depths of Truth long held, but by a few, who were capable of grasping and understanding it.

"This decade is very special in the spiritual evolvement of mankind. This is that day when Truth shall flow as a river, when the false teachings of man-made traditional idolatries will perish. False religions will be recognized for their sham by the general populace without a voice to tell them. The quickening that is taking place now within the hearts of mankind, by the Light shining within them, is beyond the greatest expectations of the Guardians of man.

"Added to this is the fact that almost 50% of the Hierarchy of this galaxy is now embodied in your midst, quietly penetrating the auric envelope of humanity's millions, letting their inner Light inundate the astral world and physical layers of the planet. No longer must enlightened souls hold their tongues, nor hide their wisdom. There is a mighty emanation of Divine frequency flowing throughout the earth, causing men's hearts to yield to their inherent spiritual instincts and responses.

"Much has been said concerning the trials and tribulations that face you in this decade, but these trials are as nothing compared to the overpowering of Spirit that will flood the earth.

"So take heart, beloved children of the stars. This is your day; this is your hour, when your words and works will dot the earth in radiance and Light and you will be scarcely able to contain your joy. We, the Spiritual Hierarchy of this solar system, have combined our own energies to send to your world a mighty spiritual outpouring that will cause your hearts to burst for joy.

"In spite of the works of darkness that will be present, in this day and this hour we promise you, the representatives of Light, a great vindication, a great victory for the God force in your midst. I am Kuthumi, and I promise you these things in the name of the Council of the Ascended Masters of the Celestial Government. As darkness deepens, so all the brighter will shine the Great Light of Our Radiant One. So shall it be."

-Tuella

Angelic being protecting a girl.

l-r: Steve Halpern, founding father of New Age music, with Publisher Timothy Beckley

INTRODUCTION

LIGHT WORKERS UNITE!

By Timothy Green Beckley

Light workers unite—the time has arrived (well almost). According to the Ashtar Command you have been born upon this planet at this specific time in order to help in humankind's spiritual development.

Some of you have arrived from a far distant star systems. Others may be reincarnated from Atlantis, Mu or Pan to assist in a cosmic plan that is long in the making.

Many do not realize yet what their assignment is, while others are just starting to see the veil lifted as their consciousness starts to expand in a more cosmic direction.

Do you feel you are an "outsider?" That something is adrift in your life, that there has to be more meaning to all of this?

Do you love nature? Animals? All of God's creations equally?

Do you see through the sinister plot by certain greedy elements of society to keep us enslaved as a species so that we can be kept under the master's thumb?

This book is not meant for everyone ‚Äì far from it! It is meant for those who feel they have been "chosen" for a mind altering opportunity that will help to lead those who are worthy to a new place among the stars.

Your time is here Starchild—REJOICE!

mrufo8@hotmail

On You Tube
Mr UFOs Secret Files

ON EARTH ASSIGNMENT: THE COSMIC AWAKENING OF LIGHT WORKERS, WALK-INS AND ALL STAR-BORN REPRESENTATTIVES

Life's Highest Loyalty

Divine Priorities

Chapter 1

Missionaries From Space

The planet earth at this time is heavily populated with Ambassadors from far flung vistas of our Universe, a vast corps of volunteers. These dedicated ones are here on heavenly assignments to aid the coming of Light and Understanding to mankind, enduring the limitations of fleshly existence to fulfill that ideal. Are you one of them?

They are the "seed souls" through whom great ideals are transferable, incorporated within creative personalities through whom the past and future become integrated. Francie Steiger has put it this way.

"Being a Star Person is possessing a Universal Consciousness; humankind's next evolutionary state of being. It is the ability to attain the perspective of one who views the planet from a Universal standpoint, understanding that all life is ONE upon its surface, interrelated and symbiotically dependent on one another, existing with a purpose as part of a Divine Plan."

Earth volunteers are programmed within their memory cells with all of the answers and directions to perform their mission successfully. How they use that power is in their hands. Only by becoming permanently embodied could we remain long enough to accomplish a meaningful mission, therefore we have laid aside the glory of other dimensions and the splendor of life as it was, before the veils were dropped upon this incognito existence.

ON EARTH ASSIGNMENT: THE COSMIC AWAKENING OF
LIGHT WORKERS, WALK-INS AND ALL STAR-BORN REPRESENTATTIVES

At this time, that encodement is pushing forward through human consciousness at an accelerated pace. As memory cells expel an inner knowingness, a tremendous planetary awakening is taking place. Your keen interest in this very manuscript is proof of your involvement. The new age movement is helping in the decodement of thousands and thousands of earth volunteers through the reprogramming made possible through programs of mediation, affirmations, readings, regressions, and knowledge. The corps of universal volunteers is intrinsically drawn to these programs and nothing can prevent their finding them as the memory cell explosion begins.

In the book, *Cosmic Countdown* by Lucy Colson, Andromeda Rex has stated,

"The 144,000 have volunteered for earth missions ever since the time when the Children of God mingled with the Children of Earth, and produced a mutant race with destructive characteristics and from your great spiritual centers many were able to make their final ascent out of earth plane. Not all of the 144,000 were on earth at once, as they are now in place around the world. Slowly they are awakening to their role and destiny in the planet's future. Within them is a 'timing device' to be triggered by a certain vibrational frequency, which eventually unfolds a quiet leadership."

Previous to this excerpt, Andromeda had mentioned that the planetary alignment of 1982 and its seven eclipse patterns had activated this mystical number of souls.

Investigation, under hypnosis, has consistently revealed a special sadness upon these souls when they enter here. Sadness at the prospect of duty on Earth is certainly understandable. Some have compared it to volunteering for service in the Marine Corps. The recruit knows it will be rough but believes that mastering the challenge will bring him maturity. The Marines build men, earth incarnation builds Masters. George Hunt Williamson has written:

"They volunteered to come to Earth and go through the reincarnation cycle here. (That means many lifetimes-Tuella) They are exactly the same as all other earthly people except for one thing. They don't belong here. They occupy physical vehicles to fulfill their missions to Earth."

ON EARTH ASSIGNMENT: THE COSMIC AWAKENING OF LIGHT WORKERS, WALK-INS AND ALL STAR-BORN REPRESENTATTIVES

This inner sadness has been reiterated by many earth volunteers. Deep within, the inner loneliness can be very intense. Unhappy love lives is a recurring characteristic, stemming from the soul's longing for its twin flame, left behind. There is often a strong recognition of other volunteers in the decodement of similar frequencies and the shared realization of strangeness in a strange place. There is a drawing toward the Spacecraft of other worlds since it was a craft such as these, which originally transported the soul to the atmosphere of earth, in preparation for its embodiment cycle.

The Commitment Crisis

At this time, the Space Commands are stepping up interaction with their incarnated representatives. There yet remains members of the fleet in this dimension, who have not awakened to that identity. The Interstellar Commands request that we lovingly share our awareness of our missions and purposes and information concerning their program for Earth, their "call to arms" to these earthbased volunteers. This book is a direct response to that call.

The term "volunteers" is valid, for each one has personally made the choice before embodiment or appearance, to respond to that clarion call. We are individually encoded to our personal assignment, and to the beings who guide us, and the group responsibilities. We are irrevocably committed in the inner levels of our being, to fulfill that mission that none other could have done as your own uniqueness would have. Most of you are now experiencing the lifting of your veils in preparation for the full recall of that which is yours to accomplish, your distinct part of the greater whole. Be not dismayed, but learn to listen, and trust as you listen. You are being guided to awareness and understanding of your individual goal in embodiment and your unique contribution of Light to the planet.

As this chapter was in preparation, Tuieta, God's Messenger from Fort Wayne, Indiana, sent us these words from Ashtar:

"We have once again begun a countdown on the number of workers of the Light Legion of Volunteers. Only approximately one third are actively involved in their commitments made prior to embodiment. An increase in the workloads of active ones is necessitated by the fact that we are working closely with the others who have chosen a less committed route.

ON EARTH ASSIGNMENT: THE COSMIC AWAKENING OF LIGHT WORKERS, WALK-INS AND ALL STAR-BORN REPRESENTATTIVES

Assignments are being increased, modified, and changed. We continually evaluate potential, as you adapt to alterations, to determine our next steps. Walk-ins from the Fleet are taking on form at this hour. You need assistance. I cannot stress enough the importance of the role each is playing in relation to the planet."

My friends, it is indeed time to awaken and acknowledge why we have come, and to be "about our Father's business." We are members of a Cosmic Family. In our agreement to come here, we agreed to be veiled. The most serious hazard we face is not preparing ourselves to fully awaken. To become so involved and caught up in earth's activities and pleasures that we lose sight of our inherent identity.

The sorrow of this day is that all too many have not yet awakened sufficiently to assume their missions in the time that remains! Many at the front lines of influence have had to undertake greater responsibilities and more extended tours of duty than originally contracted for.

Thrones Cast Down

In the Celestial Realms of our Universe, there are the thrones of four and twenty elders seated round about the great Central Sun portal and its own Great Throne Seat with its two olive trees, and the four tribal kings and queens as the ranks step down to the twenty four Elders who channel the Great Portal energies to the surrounding Universe and its galaxies. At a past time in my life, a teaching was received concerning these Great Ones:

"These are the thrones that are round about the Great Throne beyond that twelfth plane where Lord Sananda reigns. These come to Earth sometimes as great ones, sometimes as lowly ones, but always as Godly ones, and useful ones. These have important spiritual purposes, and places of appointment in the Plan, returning again and again in cooperation with that Plan. The works of these as Apostles of the Lamb, was but a portion of their works, for in many other times they have come to fulfill the needs of mankind to be revealed or given. As men and as women have they come. These higher ones come as teachers, writers, scientists, leaders, thinkers, or in whatever capacity is needed for that period in the advancement of humanity. They will all be together in this last period to inaugurate the new changes for the planet. Some have already come and gone, many others remain, and some even now will come. As the King comes, the Queen remains, or vice versa. But in this last time many will come together. These thrones are never left unoccupied; as one must incarnate, another is appointed in his stead to administer for that one."

I was further told that:

"There are twelve major seats of government upon the earth, with all others being lesser or puppet powers beneath them. The sealed ones, or earthbased volunteers, will be found scattered among those twelve nations, since enlightenment is for the entire planet. Nations who totally reject Light will be removed. It was indicated that 'when the time of sorrows' comes upon the planet, these scattered ones will gravitate to American shores; for the centering and the Administering of the Divine Plan will be America and its environs."

The Beloved Master told His band of faithful ones, that those who recognized Him would do greater works than He had done, because of His return to Celestial realms. Further, he stated that because of that inner, higher consciousness link with His Being, access to His Power would result in Greater Advancement for the Light than even He had accomplished. There is surrounded about each and every Earth volunteer, a protective presence of the forces of destiny, sometimes referred to as a "legion of angels," even as spoken of Him. As your Understanding assimilates the fact of your own Christhood, you too can do all things through that Christ within. He could control his body energy to that point of weightlessness where He could walk upon water. He could walk through solid matter through molecular rearrangement, He could eat meat, He could see all things, had awareness of all things, and spoke face to face with Angels as a daily routine.

Many, since that time, have stood in their places during the long transition to Light, when it was most difficult to do so. Many have thus come and have now gone from our midst, but you, dear reader, remain! Your battle scars are your jewels, wear them with pride. Not all of the hosts of heaven are in other dimensions; we rub elbows with them day by day. The Lord's Hosts are garbed in the flesh of sacrificial lambs of God, bleeding within, that others might find the Abundant Life.

ON EARTH ASSIGNMENT: THE COSMIC AWAKENING OF LIGHT WORKERS, WALK-INS AND ALL STAR-BORN REPRESENTATTIVES

The Memory Cells Explosion

All of us will find or have found that it is the aforementioned decoding process that throws us off balance and into a tizzy. If you are just awakening, my friend- "join the club!" It's a whirling dervish merry-go-round for your soul and you will love every minute of it.

Scattered throughout these chapters will be excerpts of my own staggering awakenings, which, in keeping with accepted protocol, exploded a bit at a time. These fragments are not necessarily chronologically organized, just shared as they come to mind. Certainly there is nothing unusual or extraordinary about my story. There are thousands just like me. Perhaps the only difference in my story is that it is being written down, it is being told, for reasons given in the preface of this book.

I speak first of all concerning a secret order of women. Late at night in November of 1984, a beautiful Egyptian female joined our meditation. She spoke:

"I am the Queen of the Nile, in the times of the worship of the One, the Source of all life, in the Symbol of the Sun. I am your friend, Nefertiti."

It was great to meet this outstanding female face to face, so to speak, and we exchanged loving greetings. She continued:

"I have other names in heaven. I use this one as an identity focus. I use it to bring into you much energy and crystallization to focus upon your crystal altar."

She went on to explain that I, Tuella, had taken an oath concerning certain information and this lifetime. It is apparently of great importance for me to remember the circle dot symbol of the sun, and a thunderbird with a pyramid behind it, "where the eyes of the Phoenix are." She explained that there was an Order, on Earth, Mars, and Saturn. Jupiter is ruler of its center with Venus watching over it. The secret Order was for the purpose of establishing Masters. They sent them to Chaldea. The masculine half of the Order sent Pythogoras, Hermes who was Thoth, and Hatton whose relationship to the Order is that of Records Keeper. A the time of this transmission, a great crystal was hanging in two zones, and energy from it was flowing to the participants.

The Order of which Nefertiti spoke, traces backward to the times before the Creation of this planet. It was these Luminaries who taught the Law of the One, and I, Tuella, had been initiated into it. Another participant clairvoyantly witnessed my being escorted by two guides to a Throne Room beneath a Sphinx, where there was music, a ceremony and an eerie sound in the passageway. Nefertiti revealed that eventually black magicians in Egypt used their power to destroy the Order, and the gates of Hell opened and something precious was lost.

"I have returned to you in this identity to awaken within you a memory of your initiation upon the planet Venus where you did take your oath and received your crown of the Phoenix as one of Our Emissaries to the Galaxy. Your many experiences on other worlds were all outer manifestations of your service to the One. In whatever culture you worked, it was ever your purpose to teach and to radiate the principles of the Law of the One."

At that point, we were honored with the visitation of another beautiful Egyptian Being, black hair, very fair, silver and gold adornment, heavy eye makeup, wearing a crown with a large circle pearl at the front, with a crystal set in a symbolic diamond.

Her power came from having learned to hold in balance the two spiritual powers, not being overcome by the darkness. Both of these ladies carried a Rod of Power.

"Therefore, my Sister, I come to you now to place upon you the Cloak of Our Order. Our Order is presently represented on Earth by eleven other women."

Further, it was explained that I had been a High Priestess of the Order of the One, and that no man would know of this Order of which Joan of Arc, Mary, and these ladies were all members. The Order was a counterbalance to the Great White Brotherhood of widely-known fame. Nefertiti continued:

"The cloak is a mantle of Our Presence and Protection. It is worn etherically and can be seen by others. To those who know, it identifies you

ON EARTH ASSIGNMENT: THE COSMIC AWAKENING OF
LIGHT WORKERS, WALK-INS AND ALL STAR-BORN REPRESENTATTIVES

as one of the twelve sisters of the Order of the One."

Then I was seen to be in a temple. A man there held out a candle to me. It does not signify any new responsibilities to those already in effect, the gesture simply acknowledges and recognizes my Authority and Responsibilities as my own. It seems that I now personally completed the circle of the twelve, all of who have now consciously been awakened to their Oath to the Law of the One. It was stated that Nefertiti at the center of the circle completes the mystical 13. Zoser and Hatton were present as representatives of the Brotherhood Order of the Phoenix.

During this session, physically my body began to manifest the actions of the ceremony. I was drawn to the floor upon my knees as the memory of the ceremony of initiation was pulled through my human consciousness. I had commented on how young I felt. The next day I was told this was because at the time the original initiation took place, I was a very young age and of short and slender stature. I had never broken the vows to serve that flame forever. They had worked with the physical to anchor the memory in this octave.

"The ability to beam the Light through your palms has never left you in this lifetime, but it has often been forgotten. Now you must remember and use its power. The raising of your right hand will cease all attacks against you, for an insignia is there that is recognizable by the dark ones, and they will not pass by mutual agreement with the Angels of Light. The marks on your palms are a symbol of Authority, which all initiates recognize. This explains why you were told recently to beam the palm of your right hand to an audience and those who saw the insignia would be healed."

I had scarcely begun to absorb this body of revelation into my consciousness when, within a week, another visitation occurred. This was another member of the Sisterhood Order of the One whose identity shall remain nameless. She is one who not only served with me as Priestess for Nefertiti, but also as a sister Priestess with me in Atlantis, as well as other continental times. I liked her statement on the topic of motivation:

"Motivation, in the fulfillment of the chosen mission, is the force that thrusts the chosen one into the task, as well as keeping that one on that pathway of service. Motivation is the force behind all dedicated and selfless service. Motivation is stored within the psyche of the Light Server from many other times of manifestation. Other lives have augmented that motivation, and the grand accumulative of its drive, propels the disciple toward destiny.

"You and I, Tuella, have the same motivation. We have served many cultures together and repeatedly taught of the ONE and His Unity within all of His Creation. We have together advanced the Law of the One whenever or wherever we have manifested Light at all. This is the fundamental basis for the Sisterhood of Light in this Galaxy, having its origin under the auspices of Lord Michael and His Knights of the Solar Cross.

"Nefertiti is known in the etherical realms as the beautiful Ascended Lady Master Venus. I come to you by her appointment to stand beside you as her emissary, representative of the entire group of twelve, of which you are One. She, herself, has served the Light upon this planet through many incarnations again and again, coming often when the need was the greatest down through the ages. Her personal vibration often surrounds you as well as the emanation of the others who labor for the One. Whether all of you shall ever meet matters not. The tie to one another is present on inner levels as each of you go your way in service. But as embodiment draws to an end for any of you, the others will be seen by that departing one, in acknowledgement.

"It has not been easy on planet Earth for women to walk as Masters, to exhibit the presence of inner Light amongst men. Nevertheless, they have come and gone, leaving their mark upon humanity, and a deposit of light in one phase of Light or another. I cite to you Madame Curie, Helena Blavatsky, Mary Baker Eddy, Florence Nightingale, Evangeline Booth, as but a few of the mystical Sisterhood of the Order of One, having taken a vow that interpenetrates every incarnation and will never be broken. You also served with Helena as the wife of one of the founders of that society. You and I, Tuella, represent a great heritage. Your own missions within the Sisterhood of older Catholicism, in other civilizations, were also an outreach of our Order for Light upon the planet. The Order has continually appeared within the Catholic Sisterhood, because in times past, it gave women a manner of living their Mastery without creating chaos. Almost every member has had times of nunnery existence behind cloistered walls. It is not the intent to identify them, but to call attention only to the difference the order has made in planetary life. Your vows to the Law of the One are embedded within your central Christed Self. This is the infallible motivation of your life. This is the purpose that burns within you. Hold high your torch and go forward holding that Light. The figure of the Goddess of Liberty that adorns the American shore, is the symbol of the Sisterhood, the Order of The One."

Oftentimes this Sisterhood is symbolized by the dove that carries an olive leaf in its beak. It may be worn as an Egyptian motif necklace or upon the breast. Monka shared these words:

"As a member of this Sisterhood, you have accumulated many sacrifices made to many planets over eons of time, over millions of years. There are 735 individual separate incarnations, that out of the other thousands, appear as shining examples which link you to the higher attributes of our Council. The symbology related to this can also be seen as the eye inside of a triangle and other symbols, which do not necessarily connotate Egypt or even Atlantis, but in fact involve many cultures spanning many star systems."

The Great White Brotherhood as well as the Spiritual Hierarchy of our Galaxy stands staunchly behind the embodied volunteer. Lord Kuthumi has been a special friend to me:

"It is I, Kuthumi, an old friend and old teacher, and one who sponsors you in this round of embodiment and service. We have many memories together from days gone by. Your work carries the mantle of my vibration to sustain and comfort and guide you through this wilderness of chaos. And so they pass before the Throne Seat, this multitude of Volunteers from every level of creation, whose desire is to have a part, whatever it might be, in seeing That Kingdom Come, and His Will be done on Earth, as it is in Heaven."

Hypnotic Research

In July of 1985, it was a privilege to have had the opportunity to cooperate with Dr. R. Leo Sprinkle, psychologist and professor at the University of Wyoming at Laramie, in hypnotic research for the retrieval of information. The recorded and documented report by Dr. Sprinkle is given here:

ON EARTH ASSIGNMENT: THE COSMIC AWAKENING OF LIGHT WORKERS, WALK-INS AND ALL STAR-BORN REPRESENTATTIVES

DR. S.: WHAT IS YOUR NAME?

ANSWER: Tuella is my name. I have come to serve humanity and the planet. I have my commitments to accomplish. I have come at this time in accordance with the needs and desire of the Hierarchy of this planet and Solar System. I am here as a helpmate to those who have also come. I am called Tuella because that is my name and has ever been my name. The earth name given to this form in the beginning was incorrect, but permitted, until that time when I COULD MANIFEST MYSELF.

DR. S.: CAN YOU SPEAK OF OR DESCRIBE ANY EXPERIENCE OF THIS ENTITY WHEN ABOARD SPACECRAFT?

ANSWER: These experiences are necessary for my continuing contact service and understanding in this dimension. I do not feel comfortable here and I must constantly refurbish and strengthen my ties with my sources to continue here. (Pause) It is my home, and I must return often, as is exemplified in the physical of this life. There is a love and longing for home. I am an alien in this land, but I must forbear, and I must continue my contacts with my home.

DR. S.: WOULD YOU EXPLAIN THE CLICKING NOISE IN HER EAR? IS IT COMMUNICATION?

ANSWER: This is again a communication device or that which works as a device, an unconscious act as far as human consciousness is concerned. It is a vital factor in my presence in this place.

DR. S.: PLEASE DISCUSS PHYSICAL AND OUT-OF-BODY EXPERIENCES ONBOARD SPACECRAFT.

ANSWER: Our term "etheric physical" is different than your physical. Our etheric physical joins with others of like being and returns to craft in most cases from which they have come. Etheric physical sees, and hears, and feels and is aware. Most times by agreement and consent, the physical consciousness is blocked from memory of these experiences. This is designated as a security procedure for the welfare of the physical embodiment.

DR. S.: WHERE IS THE ORIGINAL OCCUPANT OF THIS FORM?

ANSWER: Tuella stood by the auric field until such a time as the entity, Thelma, so, called, reached a child's consciousness and awareness. Then Tuella entered and manifested but only on the higher consciousness level, until the events of life and the time involved were proper for full manifestation of the soul entity.

DR. S.: CAN THE SOUL ENTITY TUELLA INSTIGATE CELLULAR REGENERATION TO THE HOST PHYSICAL FORM TO BETTER FACILITATE THE MISSION?

ANSWER: This process is not instigated by the soul entity, but is the result of technology and technical procedures aboard the craft of higher dimensions. This procedure has already begun within this physical form.

DR. S.: CAN YOU EXPLAIN CELLULAR REGENERATION?

ANSWER: Information concerning this technical procedure is not given to this dimension at this time. (1985)

DR. S.: PLEASE DESCRIBE THE INCIDENTS WHICH TOOK PLACE IN 1974 WHEN TUELLA AND HER TWO DAUGHTERS WERE TAKEN ABOARD A CRAFT IN OUT-OF-BODY EXPERIENCE, CONSCIOUSLY ENTERED INTO.

ANSWER: The information as given is correct. (Project World Evacuation, Inner Light, 1993) Tuella finds herself many times in an extremely large, circular, well-lighted room, surrounded by maps, diagrams, drawing of heavenly routes and lines of force. Often she is met in this great room with Athena, for it is in this room where the massive control board, in the case of Athena, is located, for the purpose of monitoring the souls of Light, on this tremendous equipment that is Athena's responsibility. Tuella stands with Athena and is shown the progress and the records of the people of this planet, whom she has come to serve and assist in their enlightenment, as an envoy and representative of responsibility from that craft.

DR. S.: EIGHTEEN DAYS AGO, TUELLA WAS RETURNING FROM OUT-OF-BODY EXPERIENCE, HEARING HER OWN SCREAMING VOICE, THEN SAYING, I WAS ON A SHIP, I WAS ON A SHIP." WHAT REALLY HAP-

ON EARTH ASSIGNMENT: THE COSMIC AWAKENING OF LIGHT WORKERS, WALK-INS AND ALL STAR-BORN REPRESENTATTIVES

PENED?

ANSWER: The experience that caused the seeming upsetting event was a return to the physical form. The experience was a pleasant one, and not the cause of the upsetting experience. It was the return to the physical that frightened the entity.

DR. S: CAN YOU DETAIL ANY RECENT OUT-OF-BODY BRIEFINGS NOT RECALLED?

ANSWER: These briefings do manifest consciously as any entity draws into human awareness the thoughts and guidance given. Guidance that is withheld and not permitted for recall is that which would disturb, upset, or cause undue anxiety to the entity.

DR. S.: WHAT IS YOUR STATUS ON OTHER DIMENSIONS AT THIS TIME?

ANSWER: I am a keeper of the records with Athena, with whom I have served and will serve again.

DR. S.: CAN YOU DISCUSS ANY DETAILS OF FUTURE MISSIONS?

ANSWER: Additional future details are released as it becomes necessary. Those who serve the planet in this manner never have withheld from them, that which is considered necessary. But information that is not relevant or related to the mission of the moment is released when needed. Entities are not "loaded" with more than is needed.

DR. S.: HAS A PHYSICAL EXAMINATION EVER BEEN GIVEN TO THIS PHYSICAL FORM BY THE EXTRATERRESTRIALS?

ANSWER: Before the final commitment of this phase, Tuella was given a total physical examination, rendered in total love, and it was determined that all physical energies were present and capable of carrying on the responsibilities. This was blocked from her memory, but took place in 1970, during one of her visits which she partially recalls. She remembers the flight observation deck, and the return. But the time upon the ship was spent in totally checking the capabilities of the entity, before the call from Ashtar was released.

ON EARTH ASSIGNMENT: THE COSMIC AWAKENING OF
LIGHT WORKERS, WALK-INS AND ALL STAR-BORN REPRESENTATTIVES

"It happened in Maryland. The appointment was made the day before. I was instructed to lie down on the floor upon a soft rug or blanket, to relax and wait for my escort. They soon came and I placed my hands upon their arms as we whizzed away into the ethers.

"From the observation deck upon the ship, I could see my inert body, which had no light. I could see Baltimore harbor and Donna in her home. My body had no light because I was not in it, they explained. I saw the dark clouds that covered New York City as we breezed by. They said Los Angeles looked the same. I remember the entry portal, the elevator and the levels that we passed on our ascent. So they blocked it out! How about that! I wonder which body they examined, the one on the floor or the one on the ship? I returned to the form very speedily because of a backache which I thought had been caused by the hard floor. Now I'm not so sure.(?) It was four months later when the call of Ashtar entered my life."

DR. S.: IS THERE ANY FURTHER COMMENT CONCERNING INTERDIMENSIONAL EXCHANGE?

ANSWER: This entity is totally committed to interdimensional exchange and lives for this purpose. No further details are needed.

DR. S.: CAN ANY TIME NOW BE GIVEN CONCERNING END TIME EVENTS?

ANSWER: As these events draw closer to reality, and the world has need of definite information, then it is the work of this entity to inform the people. We do not release this information at this time.

DR. S: DO YOU HAVE A GENERAL STATEMENT FOR THIS PERSON AT THIS TIME?

ANSWER: This entity will complete all the phases of her mission, and will remain to see the results of that labor, and then to place the foundation and formation of all labors in the responsible hands of those who will carry it on, until that time when the labor is no longer necessary to the planet.

DR. S.: WOULD YOU DESCRIBE THE E.T.'S APPEARANCE?

ON EARTH ASSIGNMENT: THE COSMIC AWAKENING OF LIGHT WORKERS, WALK-INS AND ALL STAR-BORN REPRESENTATTIVES

ANSWER: Those of the E.T. craft to whom Tuella returns are in appearance of great beauty and attractive physical form. She has on one occasion observed those of other forms who serve, but the contacts have been with those of exceeding beauty and Light in a form resembling the so-called human form but in a larger stature in the twelfth dimension.

DR. S.: DO YOU HAVE A COMMENT FOR TUELLA IN A CONSCIOUS STATE?

ANSWER: There must be a conscious continuance and irrevocable dedication to all that must be completed, regardless of obstacles and opposition. There are those who carry on. (Comments on the general mission and those who are lost to it, and weeps much in concern.) Only they have prepared for what they must do, and no other can fill their place in quite the same way. To all those who are here on borrowed energy, continue to expect that energy (Continues to weep) while there is time and before Light in its entirety is removed from the planet. For the light will cease for a time. Remain faithful, remain loyal, to the purpose for which all of you have come!

(Suggestions to return to the normal state.)

The Summons of Star Born Representatives

An oversimplified term for these individuals refers to them as "Walk-Ins." Ashtar has stated:

"This program in assisting earth is not new, however past implementations have been scattered, even rare events. But in this generation and an important point in time in the transition of earth into its new frequency, multitudes of special helpers are needed. Walk-in souls are now appearing almost daily. Their acclamation to this dimension is sometimes as drastic as the new born. They need to be discerned and assisted. A severe or devastating illness, or a tremendous healing experience may be in the record."

In an issue of our former quarterly journal, *Universal Network*, we carried an article dictated by Nathant, a representative of the Great White Brotherhood, who spoke of this phenomena.

ON EARTH ASSIGNMENT: THE COSMIC AWAKENING OF
LIGHT WORKERS, WALK-INS AND ALL STAR-BORN REPRESENTATTIVES

"When the exchange is made, often the body recovers completely but contains a new personality. The new awareness is aware of the memory patterns, which permits the recollection of all former life and environment. Therefore life can, for the most part, be resumed as permitted by the physical recovery.

"The new awareness is now possessed of a past, and conditions for an earthly environment, and the urgency of the purpose, or mission to be performed. The higher awareness decides what amount of veiling of the 'true self' is required. Also at what rate the memory of the mission and the nature of the true self can be released. Earthman would be surprised to know how many of us are among your society. Eventually you will accept it as commonplace in your existence. Each representative thus privileged must obey the same general laws in the process. The dominion of the higher awareness realizes the conscious physical organism and function in the earth environment. Veils are lifted as the new awareness senses the higher calling and pursues the purpose of the mission."

Ashtar makes clear that these representatives:

"...have a human consciousness through which they must pull their slow awareness and be helped as the infant is helped by its elders. A limited period of confusion is to be expected, but will pass swiftly with the timed release of programming within. They will find a light to guide their understanding and the early mists will clear away."

These heavy stacks of mail at *Guardian Action* headquarters are filled with letters from dear souls who are attempting valiantly to find their way through those "early mists." It isn't easy! Often the revelation can be staggering to the uninformed, and it is our hope that this book will be of help.

My own unveiling was triggered by joining the Book-of-the Month Club. Strange? Not really. Included in the six free volumes being offered were two leading books describing the life and works of Edgar Cayce, as well -as two of Ruth Montgomery's popular books. After completing the Cayce books in one day, that night I became aware of a form lying on a suspended platform, draped and totally covered in a metallic-like golden cloth. The floating form was suspended at level with my form, along the left side of my bed. Amazingly, I had no fear or anxiety, quickly associ-

ON EARTH ASSIGNMENT: THE COSMIC AWAKENING OF
LIGHT WORKERS, WALK-INS AND ALL STAR-BORN REPRESENTATTIVES

ating this sleeping form with the description of the "sleeping prophet." I simply took this as a sign to my consciousness as confirmation of a true account of this person. As I sat up on the edge of the bed following the occurrence, in deep thought concerning this and many related subjects, I received a message loud and clear. The words were, "You are a volunteer on earth assignment." At that time in my life, I did not have the foggiest idea what the words were talking about or what such a personal category might be. The "early mists" had begun. Ruth's books, in turn, led me to A.R.E. in Virginia Beach, where I then found the books of Gina Carminera. They truly triggered my understanding of reincarnation so beautifully. A 500-watt bulb lit up within my understanding and all the darkness was removed forever. It has been said that an understanding of reimbodiment is like the front steps of the Temple of Truth, and that following such an awakening, everything else falls easily into place.

Personal revelations from my own soul records quickly began to flow as the suggested routine program of meditation was set into motion. I was blessed with the opportunity for quality times of solitude each day. There followed an account which even then had staggering implications. It was the voice of Jesus Sananda:

"The ministry which is yours can be done no other way than on earth in the fleshly body. We are with you and many more of us will yet come. I anoint thee for the work that is in thy hands and I open the way to your destiny. You are one of those who come to the earth to bear heavy responsibilities. Many others will find you and know you. You are the Queen of the North Gate in heaven. You will open the Gate of the North Star for souls to enter therein. You will lead them to return to the North Gate Kingdoms which will someday be lowered to the earth. You are the queen of the North Gates and the bride of the Lion of the four. For there are four round about the throne, or four tribal Kings, and your seat is there awaiting, while you are occupied with your mission.

"Your work will be to receive and anoint those special ones who are called and are in the midst of thee. To anoint them and to seal them with the truth, which shall be their seal for the closing days. You shall know them and recognize them, for they are part of Us also, but they do not know these things. You are the queen of the North Gate and your scepter is in your hands. Did not the King of Glory appear as a lowly carpenter, unrecognized and unnoticed? So, then, how shall it be expected that they should know thee O Queen Napthali of heaven? All details and directions will be given thee as an outpost station of the Lord's Hosts. Yours is a hidden identity, not to be known but we tell thee for thy own sake to strengthen thee.

"In the latter parts of this age, the arms of darkness will seek to destroy thee, but this is not possible, for heavenly body guards surround thee. Any effort that is formed against thee will be turned into itself. You are here to give the truth in secret places to enable them to understand and to expect the things that will come. Attach not thyself any notoriety or fame of any kind that would hinder thy secret work. Such as is allowed will be permitted, but as a covering rather than an exposure of your true mission.

"You are as the television instrument which sits quietly, awaiting the hand of another to turn on the switch. This we will do when the time is prepared. The earth is a battlefield for you, away from home. You serve on foreign soil in a war that was not of your making, but you serve to bring the peace that must come. Carry on. I am Jesus Sananda."

Even though some of the content yet remains unclear, I nevertheless remember that moment as a high point in my personal devotional life and any unclear portion is held in the heart and not rejected. I have found that in time all answers do come.

You will recall that under hypnosis, Tuella explained when Thelma had reached a child's consciousness, Tuella had entered the Higher consciousness level. Interestingly enough, in 1982 a very fine channel confided to me that had it not been done in this manner, the unenlightened mother would not have been able to carry to birth the unborn Light Being.

Ashtar speaks:

"Upon entry, the High-Self Christed Being then guided the embodiment of Thelma until time and events had prepared for the ministry of Tuella incarnate-."

"Your higher spirit did descend and take control of your form at the time of your severe surgery in Maryland. This did take place during one of the nights immediately following. The delay was to determine that the form had survived."

ON EARTH ASSIGNMENT: THE COSMIC AWAKENING OF LIGHT WORKERS, WALK-INS AND ALL STAR-BORN REPRESENTATTIVES

(I clearly remember this moment in time. The icy cold had already entered the extremities of my feet and part of my legs. I called out for the nurse complaining concerning this strange coldness and its discomfort. I could read the expression on her face instantly as she ran for others to assist her. I seem to have lost consciousness briefly at that point, but soon returned all warmly snuggled in many blankets.)

Ashtar continues:

"It would not have survived had this exchange not have taken place, for the soul of Thelma was ready to depart. You are now the sole possessor of this form, you are a strong projection of the Christed Being Tuella. There has now been permission granted for a stronger force of your Being to filter through this form for the culmination of the coming public ministry. You will need a greater manifestation of memory cells awakened for the flowing into the form as a vehicle of LIGHT FOR THE PLANET. It cannot be destroyed by man, neither can it be vacated except by the granting of leave by the Great Karmic Board. It has been dedicated to the use of a representative of the Ashtar Command. Therefore, this cellular structure shall be permitted replacement with a broader spiritual encoding in its DNA/RNA functions for completion of mission in full power."

Lady Athena of the Ashtar Command has offered a few more details,

"I recall when the moment was drawing near for your supreme sacrifice to enter the vibrations of earth and the body of another, to carry on the program. Your donor gladly stepped aside according to previous agreement, being one of great love for heavenly Beings. You were our candidate to take up the task for which she had consciously prepared the psyche. Others that have entered your lifestrearn since that time have also been either walk-ins or highly placed individuals. The point in time of replacement may not yet be spoken of."

We have chosen to categorize all such information under our mental pigeonhole entitled, "mysteries that stagger." There is so much to learn, so much to know, so much to understand. Dear friends, be not dismayed by your own great revelations, seek not to confirm from others. What do they know? It is your soul that has the answers. Go within, and keep your questions before you as you await the coming of wisdom, for it will surely come to you, and when it does, it will be glorious, count on it!

The Seal in the Forehead

In the message for Jesus Sananda, he mentioned a seal, "a seal of truth, a seal for the closing days." The seal is a fascinating study topic. From the record we know that it is located in the middle of the forehead (Rev. 22:4) and shines like a star (Rev. 2:28) and that it is given to those who overcome the world, (Rev. 2:28) those who are burdened for the Light (Ezek. 9:4) This scaling is to be completed before the tribulation events upon at least 144,000 or more individuals incarnate. (Rev. 7:3, 4)

The seal represents an encompassing awareness of:

A. The spirit of God (2 Cor. 1:22)

B. The name of God (I AM THAT I AM) Rev. 3:12

C. Jesus' new name (Sananda)

D. The cities that "cometh down out of heaven" (THE GREAT MOTHER CRAFT-CITIES OF LIGHT)

E. One's own spiritual name (often with the interpretation thereof (John 1:42 and Rev. 3:12) as well as the known protection and deliverance from events at the end of this age. (Rev. 9:4)

When one comprehends all that is involved in the opening of this beautiful star (the pituitary gland) it becomes easier to grasp the concept that a new-age teacher is giving "a seal of truth, a seal for the closing days," as the Beloved Master chose to term it. This star mark of energy patterns imprinted upon the forehead are visible. Again, a quotation from the book *Cosmic Countdown* with Andromeda Rex speaking:

"Those who will be permitted to leave the planet in case of Evacuation already have a sign upon them. There is a glow just above the crown chakra and also at the Third Eye. The center of the forehead will seem to glow at times and the glow will become clearly visible to those gifted with clairvoyancy."

ON EARTH ASSIGNMENT: THE COSMIC AWAKENING OF LIGHT WORKERS, WALK-INS AND ALL STAR-BORN REPRESENTATTIVES

At an earlier session with my teachers, it was clearly indicated that this seal was related to the group we now refer to as the earth volunteers. In asking 'WHAT IS THE SEAL?" I had received this reply:

"The masses, as well as certain ones, must learn their lessons, nation as well as groups and people, things in the nature of national karma and self deeds must be met. The record must be cleared and cleansed. Those who are sealed against that day are those who are sent to comfort and teach those who must endure their lessons. The seal is their protection and armor. The seal is divinely implanted upon the soul level at incarnation, but is only known in the Christ Consciousness. It is not known in the third dimension until that time when the soul is fully awakened and enlightened. They will then know and remember their commission or at least have an intuitive feeling concerning it. It is not that they believe. It is rather that they will remember from within and will rejoice when the wisdom is recognized. The awakening or memory of the seal is the badge of discipleship in this age. These will be given to know their Universal Names, this is the seal, to know purpose, to know person, and to know the plurality of personalities. Gradually the seal of each will unfold, through guidance, meditation, revelation or inner conviction. Those not of the sealed number will scorn and reject, for how can they accept that which, to them, does not exist? Later they may become followers of the sealed ones, but not a part of the active working score, the 144,000 who must be sealed before the cleansing can begin."

Through Nada-Yolanda of MARK-AGE (P.O. Box 290368, Ft. Lauderdale, Florida 33329) we have a part of a Hierarchical announcement:

"We have been in the midst of the War of Armageddon for a long time. There is not one of us who cannot read the signs of the times, the marks of this age. That is why we are linked together as a network of Light workers. No matter how fractured and destructive individuals and groups throughout the planet seem to be, we cannot lose sight of the fact that millions of souls have at least the awareness of a New Age, plus a strong personal desire to express a higher consciousness and mastery over this dimension. Never lose sight of the fact that we are one in our struggle, with coworkers and allies of various backgrounds and activities.

"The hierarchy of Ascended Masters is informing all of us that we have established a new beachhead, a new octave of spiritual energies from which to function. We never are given more than we can handle; and we always receive good training by our own I AM Self before every challenge occurs, in order for us to be victorious."

Telling It Like It Is

It is an irrevocable spiritual principle that we must share our personal experiences because they will trigger another soul. The sharing of one individual can set into motion the awakening of another. The experience of one may quicken into participation; another who hesitates along the wayside, who fears the unknown journey or uncharted sea, yet secretly, desperately longs to begin that journey.

The late Gutzon Borium was the distinguished sculptor who carved out of the rocky mountainside of Black Hills, South Dakota, the most stupendous memorial on earth. However, his greatest work is considered to be the head of Lincoln in the Washington capitol. Its block of marble had long been in his studio. Into that studio each morning came an old lady to clean the place. She was used to the marble block and for many days hadn't noticed it. One day in astonishment and terror, she saw the unmistakable lineaments of Abraham Lincoln. She asked the secretary, "Is that Abraham Lincoln?"

"Yes," said the secretary. "Well," asked the old lady, "how in the world did Mr. Borium know Abraham Lincoln was in that piece of stone?" Dear Ones, it is the vision of our unseen capabilities, the inner splendor of our Christhood, which attracts the invisible guidance to our side.

The inevitable termination of my dull and uneventful first marriage was a crucial time in my young adult life. This relationship with an intellectual genius of around 160 IQ had served only to awaken my mind and the pursuit of mental activity. This was apparently a step toward the future. My little tot and I were living with my grandmother.

At that rather crucial event in time, an aware person spoke to me of their relationship to a Heavenly Father. His place in all things and such matters. The words spoken are not as significant in memory as the manner of absolute assurance with which they were spoken. For the first time in my life I became conscious of an unknown hunger within. In the moonlight that night, I sat upon a blanket beneath my grandmother's cherry trees and looked up toward the sky. I had no religious training of any kind.

ON EARTH ASSIGNMENT: THE COSMIC AWAKENING OF LIGHT WORKERS, WALK-INS AND ALL STAR-BORN REPRESENTATTIVES

I did not know how to frame a proper prayer. I didn't know just how I was to approach this thing which I very much desired to do. Finally, I simply spoke out loud, a bit desperately, "If there's anybody up here, if anybody's listening or anybody cares, I'd like to talk to you." Awkward? Yes. But the sincerity of that first call resonated throughout the Universe. "God ... I know I'm on the outside of something I don't know anything about ... but ... please God ... I want to be taken in. I can't handle this ignorance. I want to know things, but most of all I want to know You. 99

I kept looking skyward, through my tears, then relaxed and closed my eyes. I sensed someone standing beside me, and thought it was my grandmother in her nightgown. As I started to open my eyes, I saw the many folds of the hem of a full garment, and sandeled feet beneath it. In startled wonderment, I realized that some angelic being had stood beside me in answer to my call. I had been heard! Someone had listened and an inner knowing assured me that I had been 'taken in' like some lost straying creature that appears suddenly on one's doorstep. That moment in time was the catalyst that generated an ongoing glory of spiritual adventure that has never ended. '

The Glory Road

My second marriage led me through the rural ranchlands of Texas where the quietness and seclusion greatly contributed to soul development, triggered awareness and expanding growth. I began a ministry of spiritual counseling and prayers by mail which I called Soul Clinic. It expanded to become a monthly devotional journal. Faced with my responsibilities to my home and babies, I simply began where I was, doing what my hands found to do. This is an excellent place to begin, regardless of what any future mission might be. I recall one day, after depositing spiritual help in my mailbox for some distant needy soul, and beginning the long hot trek back to the house over the dusty drive, I whispered, "I wish I could do more." I was frozen in my tracks when a loud audible voice seemed to shout from right above my head, "You shall have your wish."

At that point in my life, I also learned to participate in spiritual warfare. My youngest baby was born with asthmatic tendencies and, for a long period of her infancy, had to be held up at night to prevent choking and loss of breath. It was those long hours through the night that afforded me so much time for study and spiritual pursuits. I read the scriptures through eight times from cover to cover, which later proved to be a genuine investment in future usefulness. In the dead of night, as I had gently placed the child back in her crib, I sensed the presence of some thing or someone awfully evil standing in the doorway. I said with a feeling of great repugnance: "What do you want?" IT said, "I have come to get your baby." That did it! I swung around to place myself between IT and the crib. Shaken but determined, I shouted "In the Name of Jesus the Christ, you shall not touch this child!" He just looked at me. I countered again with a command for IT to leave my home, my property, and my life and to go in the name of Jesus from this place and never to return. "Now ... GO!" Then it was gone.

There have been many other attempts, attacks of the dark ones. Once as I drove along a mountainside road where the right side was a sheer drop down, something, a power, or someone, tried to get control of the steering wheel. Audibly I went through my protective ritual and denouncement of interference which eventually succeeded, but in the meantime I had to physically use all of my strength to wrestle the wheel back into my control. Such is the life of the spiritual warrior, only usually in a much more insidious vein. The trick is to learn to look behind the human involved or the seeming earthly circumstance and to recognize the stamp of the opposition behind the visible situation, then deal with the source!

Events of life much later led the family to New York State. It was there, during intense devotional experiences, that a clear call to a definite public ministry came through. At that place and point in time, when such a thing was almost unthinkable for a woman, the unmistakable message came, "Thou shalt be a great prophet unto me.

It was very confusing to me. It was difficult to reconcile the peculiar wording with my traditional concept of the ministerial calling ... which in itself was difficult enough to grasp and accept.

After a few weeks of this wrestling with terminology and concepts, I asked straightforward, "Lord, are you calling me to... preach?" No answer. Instead a vision. I was shown a long, narrow and very stony road. The kind of terrain where you would want an inch thick rubber sole to even enter it. Really awful. At some points, the road became but a path blended with the mountainside. Not just rocky and rough, but jagged and sharp stones that could cut through that inch thick sole. I thought about that road for several days ... seeing almost nothing else. Then, it came, while looking down that road, His Voice, "Would you follow Me down that road?" I didn't know.

ON EARTH ASSIGNMENT: THE COSMIC AWAKENING OF LIGHT WORKERS, WALK-INS AND ALL STAR-BORN REPRESENTATTIVES

I had to think through the answer before I gave it. I didn't know whether He could depend on me or not. I thought He was taking a chance. Finally after severe sifting as wheat from chaff, and clearly aware of the implications of my commitment, I answered Him, "Yes Lord ... I will follow you." He said, "Even though that road may be rough-and rocky-and weariness beset your pathway?" (A stickler for details, Our Lord!) From deep within a bosom sopping wet with tears, I responded, "You know me Lord, I've made up my mind. I'll follow you!"

It became a glory road. We walked together. And He had a way of keeping me floating off the ground so that I never felt the pain, or jabs, just kept close behind Him. I signed up immediately for the long course of study that led to ordination. The head honcho of our District jibed, "I'll never be able to place you!" I looked him in the eye with, "You won't have to, the Lord'll do it." I became the district Sunday replacement, driving hundreds of miles each Sunday to fill empty pulpits while the men were away. The fun thing was that when these places became vacant, guess who was invited to fill them? The head honcho had no problems at all.

When Sunday school enrollment doubled, and church membership greatly increased, with my salary raised twice, the congregation voted me a three year recall. This was an unprecedented vote of confidence for any pastor and a mandate to the district not to disturb their leadership. I had earned the right to be the first woman in the Hudson Bay area to hold such a post. He jumped on the bandwagon so to speak, and appointed me as District Director of children's societies, chaplain of the girl's camp, camp meeting children's worker, and District Delegate to the National Convention, with all expenses paid. I had found that every step I took along that rocky road, the Divine bulldozer had been there before me to smooth the way.

A severe physical disability entered my husband's life, and I was faced with providing the family support. Thus my service as home missionary provided housing and income for my family's needs, while affording me the opportunity to fulfill my commitment to spiritual goals.

There were many visions in those days. One in particular seemed to haunt me. I had climbed the winding stairway of a high tower, and arrived at its uppermost room. I opened the door and saw within me, at the center, an empty chair, and an opened window. At the uppermost part of this high tower, I went in and sat on the chair. I later learned that the chair represented the Spirit of God. An ongoing conviction within, aroused me to an awareness that there was more to go on to, that I had only just begun. I was instructed to read Genesis. I didn't know why, or where to begin ... so I started at the beginning. I read as far as the second verse which was saying, "God's Spirit moved upon the waters." And then it came, the Loving Still Small Voice from within announcing to me, "As my Spirit moved upon the waters ... so shall I move upon souls for thee." It was a moment when all of the fountains of the great deep were broken up within, when the windows of heavens were opened upon me, and I knew this was an anointing for something that was yet to come. I wrote out my commitment in longhand which I have to this day:

"Lord, I give up all of my own purposes and plans, all of my own desires, hopes, and ambitions, and accept all of Thy Will for my life. I give myself, my life, my all utterly to Thee, to be Thine forever. I hand over to Thy keeping all the people whom I love, who will take second place in my heart. Fill me and seal me with Thy Holy Spirit. Work out Thy Whole Will in my life, at any cost, now and forever. For me to live is Christ and to die is gain."

The Separated Life

The truly enlightened soul exhibits inherent and natural characteristics of a broad tolerance for other children of the Creator, regardless of the belief patterns involved. An insight born within me, knew there must inevitably be a common ground for unity and oneness between us all, even though any practical expression of that attitude consistently created enmity toward me on the human level. My distress increased.

The competitiveness and ill will exchanged between the many segments of Orthodoxy sickened my soul, and I became more and more uncomfortable being a part of it. I clearly perceived the errors and pitfalls of human divisions, polarizing rules, crystallization of creeds and the high politics of organized churchianity. I learned to "hang loose" in my tolerance, and with an honest humility, pursued the literatures of the great world religions and the New Age writers. Step by step, an unseen guidance beamed revealing Light upon every form of human prejudice. As the little child clings to the sides of his playpen or the rounds of his walker-he does not truly walk alone until he no longer leans upon these. So it is that the sincere seeker of truth must learn to walk the pathway alone, beyond all support of humanly engineered dogmatic ideologies. We have not reached that high plateau as long as we lean upon these things. Ecclesiastical cannibalism and man's inhumanity to man, within the confines of bigotry, is frightening to behold. The clearing out of all of these old patterns is a first step away from the old dimension of life.

The experience of widowhood combined with personal health problems, catalytically converged on my departure from the formal ministry. With relentless enthusiasm, I plunged into a deeper search for truth. It was into this setting that the four books previously described in this book, were placed in my hands, for the triggered, decoding that followed.

The finding and sharing of all truth is indeed a Divine priority of life on this planet, calling forth life's highest loyalty, to our Radiant One.

ON EARTH ASSIGNMENT: THE COSMIC AWAKENING OF
LIGHT WORKERS, WALK-INS AND ALL STAR-BORN REPRESENTATTIVES

The Star-Born Child

Life's Highest Commitment

The Divine Program

Chapter 2

The Council of Cosmic Causation

There is Divine Order in all of Creation. At the massive vortex portal, which we call the Great Central Sun, there the Throne described in Revelations is located. It is the seat of Divine Government, surrounded by those we call the Celestial group. From the Center of All That Is, wherein resides the Unpronounceable, beyond dimensional existence, that massive Golden Portal provides for the combined regions of the Omniverse, including our own Universe.

Just as a shaft of Light, shining through a prism, splits twelve different rays, so Lord Michael, the Throne Beings, and the twenty four Elders that encircle the Throne area, constitute a prism for this unfathomable vortex of energy to disperse into 12 regions of the Cosmos.

Lord Michael is an example of one of the many who was given charge of the creative forces, to create immortal Beings with the capability to understand the Almighty One. From the highest level, One oversees all subdivisions. From the Great Cell it subdivides into various systems. On the zodiacal basis, systems of 12 were expanded with various systems representing influences and emphasis. However Monka has explained:

"Astrology of today is all that is left of a celestial government bringing order out of chaos in the Universe. Astrology once charted a system of Light symbols like a great diamond. These became 12 rays, 12 houses of our Lord, but when Astrology passed beneath the waters, only a fraction,

ON EARTH ASSIGNMENT: THE COSMIC AWAKENING OF
LIGHT WORKERS, WALK-INS AND ALL STAR-BORN REPRESENTATTIVES

a small fragment, of the knowledge was passed down."

In our world, it's symbology remains in the 12 petaled lotus flower, Stonehenge, the 12 radiating arms of Osiris-all symbols of the God's given charge of this system.

There exists beyond the so-called 12th plane, beyond the context of dimensions, at the highest point on a totally unphysical plane, these pure energy, incorporeal Beings, partially manifest, Immortals who dwell in the soul essence, sometimes called the Guardians, the Elohim, the Angels or the Old Ones. From this Celestial Station, they oversee the functioning of our physical worlds, instituting changes that are in accord with Divine Plan. This Celestial Group includes the four and twenty elders "round about the Throne clothed in white Raiment and on their heads crowns of gold."

(An interesting sidelight of information was shared concerning the entire Throne and Celestial Group. I was told that, with the exception of only a few, from the beginning of the Divine Program until the end of the present tribulation period, all of them will have laid down an embodiment in martyrdom on earth at least once.)

They are, in reality, 12 pairs of Beings, not 12 of each polarity, but 24 Androgynous Beings, each containing -within themselves the expression of balance for both. These "Elders" are channeling units, focusing the force that radiates outward, that creates and maintains Universes. They are the primary receivers of instruction from the Radiant One, Omnipresent, Infinite, as if all were one consciousness.

They are perfectly capable of placing their thoughts into the minds of chosen ones through telepathy or whatever method they choose. The Celestial Group are they who have manifested the Universe, its galaxies, its systems, its inhabitants. They are instruments of expression of spiritual laws, not subject to man's desires or the need of free will.

Visualize, then, this Great Central Sun, encompassed by these 24, representing this center protective ring of Luminosity, even as the brightness of our physical sun hides the portal that is beyond it. There are 12 divisional regions that are round about the circle of these 12 Regents and the Consorts, radiating as 12 spokes. These 12 rays radiate outward establishing the Cosmic Sphere, these 12 emanations of the Infinite One working out into these rays of collective consciousness referred to as Brotherhoods, Sisterhoods of Light. This is the Great Golden Light coming through the Throne Seat and down through its channels. This is the COUNCIL OF COSMIC CAUSATION.

The Cosmic scheme of government is not a government of people, but a governing of FORCES and an application of the 12 Laws of Creation. Monka continues:

"We constantly seek to cooperate with the rules of these Ancient Ones, these Elder Ones, the Elohim, for these are the ones who breathed the Ineffable Name in the 12 Seed Symbols, which, when seen as a great geometrical pattern, can be conceived as a crystal of many facets. The four and twenty Elders that surround the Throne Seats, have sometimes been called Angels by men; a word that simply means messenger. These are much more than that."

The Interdimensional Federation of Free Worlds

Thus, we see, radiating outward form these 12 pairs of Sovereign Ones, the 12 rays of expanding Light going out to the 12 regions of the Cosmos at this 12th dimensional point, which makes up the highest beings of representation of the Universal Government, which, combined, make up what is called the Interdimensiorial Universal Federation.

Each of the 12 regions of the Federation are individually governed by a Command, headed by a Supreme Commander, whose responsibilities encompass Universes, and all of their Galaxies, Solar Systems and Planetary bodies within each region. Directly in jurisdiction over these 12 Commands and their regions are four Sovereigns, symbolized in Revelation 4: 6,7, as four "living creatures" represented as a Lion, an Eagle, a Sun and a King. These four, often referred to by Bible scholars as the "four Tribal Kings," hold jurisdiction over 3 regions each, of the 12. Thus there are what is sometimes termed 12 Spiritual Nations, or 12 Houses, or 12 Gates. Three to the east, three to the west, three to the north, three to the south, of the celestial, leading into the 12 regions.

Thus, each trinity of Commands are gathered into four combined Forces known as the Lion Force, the Eagle Force, the Sun Force and the Royal Force, representing a United Force for the benefit of all. Millions of personnel and craft from incredibly far distant space, make up the United Cosmic Force.

But above and beyond the four Sovereign's, with their 12 Supreme Commanders, we have the Elders of the Celestial Group who stand at the doorways into each of those regions of Cosmos. Lord Jesus Sananda and His Queen consort, stand at the door of our Region of the Cosmos, as our Vortex of the Lord Michael energies through the Great Central Sun Portal of the Unmanifest Radiancy of the Creator Energies. Ashtar places Lord Jesus Sananda as our ELDER BROTHER, of the Celestial Group of Elders, existing above and beyond out-of-context with dimensions. Other higher Space Beings (so-called) refer to Lord Jesus Sananda as a Celestial, not from a certain place or planet.

I am thrilled when I recall His Words, "I Am the Door, no man cometh to the Father except by Me." For he is the Doorkeeper for this Cosmic region, into the Celestial realms. No wonder He said, "I, if I be lifted up, will draw all men unto Me."

The Galactic Confederation

The seat of government for our local Vega Galaxy is located in the Pleiades star cluster of systems. They were its first colonizers, and the foreparents of our Solar System, of which Earth is a part. The Galactic Confederation Council on the Pleiades, represents three and-a-half million craft with thirty percent on constant standby and control of Ashtar, Supreme Commander for our regional area of the Cosmos patrolled by the Ashtar Command.

The Solar System

The governing seat of our local Solar System is located on planet Saturn, headed by the Saturnian Council. Lord Monka not only represents our Solar System to the higher Galactic Confederation, but he also acts as representative of planet Earth on the Saturnian Council, since we are still too far behind in spiritual development to warrant our own representative.

I was wondering why the Commands were releasing this kind of information at this time, and Ashtar replied:

ON EARTH ASSIGNMENT: THE COSMIC AWAKENING OF LIGHT WORKERS, WALK-INS AND ALL STAR-BORN REPRESENTATTIVES

"When the seeded people are exposed to these things, it will prepare them for the shock of the Universe, from which they have come. This species seems to think it evolved upon this orb. Yet, in reality, you come from many places in the heavens, your citizenship is from anywhere in the Cosmos. When you go outside at night, and look up at the sky, you could point your finger and say, 'I've been there!'...and you would be perfectly correct. You are not consciously equipped to remember these things, but they are true. All we can do on behalf of enlightenment is prod your memory, and, ultimately, it is your free will to accept or deny it."

So, friend, if the record shows that you spent 500 years on the planet Korendor 25,000 years ago, take it in stride. Some of us have been around and around and around-for a very long time. We have been born again ... and again-and again ... just trying to be helpful!

(All of the facts and information given on these pages were jointly given by Ashtar and Monka.)

We have now spiralled our chapter down to where we live on one small planet, upon which the eyes of the entire region, and perhaps even a few from the other eleven areas of the Cosmos as well, are focused with such interest.

Those of us with knowing hearts, aware of the vastness of the big picture of the structure of Universal Worlds, with our encoded propensity to grasp its truth, smile quietly upon those who exhaust themselves continually seeking physical proof of such.

UFO Research

Have you ever seen a dog chasing its tail? Do not laugh. He is deadly serious in his endeavor. He has an end in view. He has a planned approach, he'll go, around in circles. The problem is that he can never catch up with that end, because when he arrives where he thinks he is, its elsewhere. In fact, it's way ahead of him! The fact is, if he would just be still and quiet himself, he could reach that end which he seeks.

Speaking of UFO researchers, so-called-I use the word loosely -for such activity is neither science nor research, generally financed for

ON EARTH ASSIGNMENT: THE COSMIC AWAKENING OF
LIGHT WORKERS, WALK-INS AND ALL STAR-BORN REPRESENTATTIVES

general propaganda or a hideaway self-created. For when you research something, it is proof or evidence, that there is something you do not know. It is an activity a bit like trying to capture human breath and measure it to prove it exists and then bottle it up to sell to people who cannot breathe anymore. Well, they wouldn't need it anyway.

So you research what you either do not know or refuse to believe. If I do not know something, the research possibilities are endless. They need never stop. Because, if I do find something of pertinent or factual nature, it would be tossed aside or buried in a hole. Why? Because evidence unaccepted upsets the mind set, making it necessary to rationalize it away or start another research society.

The great crowd of unbelievers have to follow someone, so they follow the researchers down the cloudy path. They consume book after book of facts and photographs and happenings by the carload, and become experts or walking encyclopedias on the subject, to remain comfortable with their unbelief, because they seek with the intellect, and they seek outside of themselves.

The greatest astronomer and cosmic scientist of our day, whose name is a household word, insists there is no life on other worlds, yet ... how many of you KNOW you are from another world? Science has been unable to prove the Presence of god, yet ... how many of you have personally experienced the I AM PRESENCE OF GOD WITHIN? Are you waiting for the researchers to confirm it? How many of you visit other planets, other words, Mother Ships, and converse with Higher Beings, while your body sleeps? The scientist could scientifically measure the heat of the mattress capturing the warmth of your form-that's right! They could measure how long it took the pillow indentation to rise or the wrinkles to level out. They could have a big time-chasing their tails, that's right! They would logically prove behind a shadow of a doubt it could not be done-yet beloved-you and I do it all the time. That's right. We just let it happen.

FOR THE ONLY WAY TO KNOW A SPIRITUAL TRUTH IS TO EXPERIENCE IT AND MAKE IT A PART OF YOUR BEING. You incorporate it into your body of Truth ... not through seminars, not through classes, not from channeling, not from the facts of research, but you will know that you know that you know WHEN IT HAPPENS TO YOU! In the voice of science-in the stillness of the inner citadel of Being—in the sacred closet of the Great Light

ON EARTH ASSIGNMENT: THE COSMIC AWAKENING OF LIGHT WORKERS, WALK-INS AND ALL STAR-BORN REPRESENTATTIVES

YOU will know.

It has been said that it only takes one white crow to prove that all are not black! Carl Sagan's research is spending millions and millions of our tax dollars with their tremendous electronic gear, just to get a word, a peep, a grunt ... from outer space! But, my friend, as you rest there quietly with this book in hand, with no one to see you but the entire Universe(!), if I were to privately ask you, have you ever experienced the unspoken words of a Being from other dimensions, or Outer Space, or a scout ship, or a craft far away in the solar system, or this galaxy or other galaxies of the far-flung universe, would you just sneak your hand up a little bit to admit, "Father, I have." And as all of you are reading and responding to this ... then I say, "Dear Father-LOOK THEM OVER!"

Or perhaps your quivering soul is just now stirring into an awareness of Cosmic revelation. Perhaps you are just now standing on the threshold of finding out who you are, why you are here and what your mission to this planet might be. Then you can slip your right hand up as well and think/speak your words, "No, I never have, but by the Grace of God and the help of my Guardian Band, I will follow my heart until it DOES happen to me!" Alright!

The Discipline of Delay

Heaven prompts and prods and calls, and the awakened Volunteer runs and runs to respond and prepares to cooperate ... and then has to stand and wait just like the old Army days, you hurry up and wait. What's going on here, you say? What's the matter? Why isn't everyone dragging me into their groups to speak? Why aren't they forcing their mailing lists into my hand? Why isn't the money rolling in to pay for this great mission I have to give to the world? Why do not the doors open, I'm pushing on them hard enough?

Or perhaps one who has received loud and clear facts and material concerning the Evacuation, becoming well versed on the philosophy, the details, the magnitude of it ... wonders, "Why didn't it happen yesterday? What about Sunday? Or maybe next Tuesday morning-at 9:00 o'clock?" They bruise their fists upon the gates of heaven demanding dates, times, details, results.

ON EARTH ASSIGNMENT: THE COSMIC AWAKENING OF
LIGHT WORKERS, WALK-INS AND ALL STAR-BORN REPRESENTATTIVES

One could cut a lovely rosebud, and in impatience to see its fullest bloom, tear it to spread outward. There might be a semblance of its coming beauty, but one would have destroyed what might have been, had God's soft raindrops expanded its heart and His warm sunlight opened each petal in its special place, at the time right, in perfect hue. For there is a, time, a season, for everything under the Sun, ere the Divine Program be sabotaged. Thus-we wait-for our personal trumpet to sound.

Those who guide us, make no mistakes, neither are they ever too late, for all things are given ... within God's time. You may feel ready with what you have to give ... but perhaps hearts are not readied to receive. Consider that God's most beautiful fruits ripen in the shade. The grace "to do" what we must do flows easily. The grace "not to do" is harder to come by, but it builds Masters.

Hatton speaks:

"One major concern is holding our key persons steady on their course. The uncharted seas of the new program means they must be poised and calm in their steadfastness. They are our foundation and our base of operations. All will come to pass when all things are right. In our higher positions of authority, neither can we state time schedules, nevertheless we carry on our affairs and assignments with regularity and dependability.

"We too are committed to a cause from which there is no turning back. We who array for battle must also be a part of the waiting, knowing there is Divine Order in all things."

A Prophetess and Her Peers

In time the decoding and directives that have exploded within inner levels of the Earth Volunteer, will be acknowledged and honored by their peers.

The publishing of Kuthumi's golden book, *"World Messages for the Coming Decade"* opened doors for seminars in Arizona. The release of the first edition of *Project World Evacuation* in 1982 (since updated by Inner Light in 1993), led to my having a part in the program of the 21st Space Age Convention at Reno, along with ten male authorities on the New Age.

ON EARTH ASSIGNMENT: THE COSMIC AWAKENING OF
LIGHT WORKERS, WALK-INS AND ALL STAR-BORN REPRESENTATTIVES

As I was leaving the platform, Reverend Wayne S. Aho, President of the New Age Foundation, approached and asked me to remain. He addressed the audience to explain a newly-organized "Peer Awards Recognition Program," the Foundation he had launched.

Wayne Aho was an Officer in Army Intelligence in World War II, a deeply spiritual and brilliant man; his burden for our civilization and the Divine Program for the planet, were reflected in his words:

"In the assignment of many New Age individuals of raising earth consciousness, at a time when the world would appear bound for its own destruction with ever greater war plans and weaponry, an intercession has become apparent, known to countless individuals. Help has come from those ... not of earth, from various regions of Space. This, in addition to those who reside on other realms, or dimensions. A grand transition has been underway, especially in the last 35 years, since the first nuclear bombs were dropped on Nagasaki and Hiroshima, Japan by the United States, toward the end of World War II.

"Regardless of official pressures and deceptions, disinformation from agencies charged with the public interest, and often a hostile press, there are those on earth who have served diligently and well. This service, or giving of one's self, time and even endangerment to survival has continued. Thankfully, we can say the world is changing, albeit not as rapidly as one would hope. The danger of nuclear conflict, or an accident of momentous nature, is mounting each day, even as warned by Orfeo Angelucci in *Secret of the Saucers* many years ago.

"The New Age Foundation Inc. has been encouraged to issue certain awards and recognition for this faithful service on the part of so many. Included are some who are unknown, as their sacrifice and service is not known to the world. Earth tends to build the statues and memorials long after worthiness was proved, and the recipient of any given honor is gone from this dimension. There are countless examples of this, even in this generation. We could name such as Nikola Tesla, who introduced this electrical age, Dr. Karl Reich, Rudolf Steiner and many others. Since we recognize more than one science in the experiences of life, it is important to give recognition in Spiritual and Mind as well as the physical sciences. What happens in mind sciences does not manifest on the physical level till long afterward. One example is the comic strips or "funny papers," which intrigued

ON EARTH ASSIGNMENT: THE COSMIC AWAKENING OF
LIGHT WORKERS, WALK-INS AND ALL STAR-BORN REPRESENTATTIVES

many of us as youngsters. The exploits of such as Flash Gordon and Buck Rogers cannot now be reported. It has become 'TOP SECRET' in present and future war weaponry. In this perilous time, it is expedient that awards be given to those working for consistency, hope, love, and survival of the species, as so many are involved in the destructive war plans.

"The hope is that the great awakening, now underway, will shift the direction of our civilization toward constructive sciences.

Why attempt to save the lives of little children, overcome sickness and disease while the course of the great nations is to wipe out millions in senseless mass destruction.

"These awards have been encouraged by those who serve 'on high, who watch over and assistant earth man in all possible ways."

He then graciously, as a complete surprise, presented me with a Certificate of Merit and an Award for Outstanding Service to Humanity.

It is comforting to know your work and mission, but it is joy unspeakable to know it is recognized and appreciated by your peers. The motto of the New Age Foundation aptly states, "That which challenges the thinking of one generation becomes the acceptance level of the next.

Reverend Aho has compiled a fact sheet of UFO information from worldwide sources since Nagasaki, Hiroshima and World War 11, based on his some 30 years of studies. In the interests of the Divine Program and the preservation of his work, we quote his Fact Sheet verbatim:

"Although sightings go back to the earliest language on earth, Sanskrit, and reports by major religions, this report will deal most directly with the modern era. A good source of information for earlier periods may be found in the *Encyclopedia Brittanica*, Roman and Greek history, and reports carried by historical legends. It has been revealed that the sailing crews of Christopher Columbus saw strange craft, as well as Thor Heyerdahl, who crossed the Atlantic by raft.

"1. We have selected Nagasaki and Hiroshima as the key beginning moment for this data, as statistics show that after the first nuclear weapons were exploded over these cities, UFO sightings increased by millions of percent all over the world. Each one can arrive at their own reason for this. One conclusion is that intelligent cultures now realized earth is on a course of self-destruction. The earth may have been declared a disaster area by intelligences more advanced than the earth.

"2. Sightings have been continual and varied. They have included every country of the world. It finally arrived at a point where the smallest country in the world, Granada, requested public hearings in the United Nations General Assembly. Many sightings had occurred in Granada.

"3. The type of people who have seen a UFO is a cross-section of every trade or strata of life on the earth. No one has been left out. Those in academic fields, or legislators, have been cautious about reporting experiences, due to the fear of losing jobs or elections. Unfortunately, ridicule has interfered with honest research.

"4. Photos have come from all over the world, depicting craft unknown to our current earth science. Almost without exception, there are no wings or tail assemblies. The craft vary in size and shape. Some are discs, others cigar-shaped or elliptical. Well over 40 types have been described or photographed; there may be thousands. Many photos have been carefully checked and authenticated. Radar reports in many cases coincide with sightings or photos. Usually, there is no sound in flight.

"5. Personal experiences vary as much as the sightings. Many experiences have been witnessed. The movie *Close Encounters of the Third Kind* depicted some of the types of experiences. I have found that close encounters can be unique and different, geared to the individual involved. Many have been given warnings for the good of humanity, indicating that our warring and destructive trends can lead to disaster. Many have reported tremendous feelings of friendship and concern, even love of mankind from beings involved.

"6. Secrecy has continually shrouded the UFO question and is still in force. UFO groups have reached the level of the Supreme Court with a request for secret Air Force files, under the Freedom of Information Act. Even at that stage, the question is not being resolved. Former Presidents have promised in campaigns they would open the secret files on UFOs to the public. The promises were not fulfilled.

"7. Pertaining to secrecy, Congressman John Moss of California was led to shed light on this problem after 18 years in the House of Representatives. 'I have discovered that the main amount of funds spent on security is not spent to keep information from an enemy, that would give aid and comfort to the enemy; rather, it is spent to keep information from the American taxpayer, that would give aid and comfort to the taxpayer.'

"Dr. James McDonald, University of Arizona, discovered an order from the CIA to the Air Force to ridicule all UFO sightings. He published it. It was then reclassified 'Top Secret.'

"Do the war planners of this nation, or any nation on earth, have the spiritual, social, philosophical understanding to determine the DESTINY and SURVIVAL of the human race on earth? What is your conclusion?

"Norman Mayer may be the first victim of an ever-growing nuclear monster which, according to nuclear scientists, is 'out of control.' The question will continue to pervade our consciousness: what possessed one man, unarmed with no apparent hostile intent toward the nation or the human race, to take on the aligned thought forms of 'establishment thinking' on the nuclear issue?

"I learned in intelligence school as an officer in Army Intelligence, WW II, that it was important, in solving any intelligence question, to not ignore one small particle of information. I have problems even now of whether to throw away small scraps of paper, notes accumulated in New Age, UFO and Space Research. In going over accounts of the life and attitude of Norman Mayer, ONE ITEM especially stood out to me as that important point to heed. He warned other nuclear protesters they were not moving fast enough! Was he privy to a realization of coming catastrophe, unless we, as a civilization, make an abrupt turn?

"I am reminded that when the controversy arose whether a high altitude nuclear blast should be set off high over the Pacific Ocean, many scientists, including Van Allen, who was credited with discovery of the Van Allen belt, said it would do no harm. The reason for this 'test' high above the earth has never been adequately explained; why did we take the risk? The damage done to earth and its environment from this 'mistake' has never been explained further. It was not till years later that Boeing engineers announced in anger that 'we had changed the Van Allen belt for perhaps millions of years. Future astronauts would now have to cope with radiation which had not been there.' What was the full measure of damage? Will we ever know? How many have the real facts, wherein nuclear war is concerned, be it limited or a holocaust? History may prove Norman Mayer absolutely right in his premonition and apparent hysteria.

"I am reminded that when nuclear testing was conducted on the Nevada desert, the level of atmospheric radiation in Los Angeles arrived at the level of 'critical.' There was one more test scheduled.

Although the Mayor of Los Angeles protested bitterly, attempts continued to set off one more blast. Then, the predetermined level of what was labeled 'critical' was doubled. Now, official sources announced, it was not critical any more. We have doubled the level. Wilbur Smith, renowned Canadian scientist who worked on the Top Secret AVRO CAR project, a joint attempt by the U.S. and Canada to build a 'flying saucer,' even while governments were officially denying there is any such thing, revealed the following information: He had developed a system of communication with occupants of flying saucers. They told him, Had they not cleansed our skies of radiation from atomic weapons testing, millions of our people would now be dead! Further, they communicated to him, if he cared to observe one of their craft dumping radiation waste into a volcano near Ottawa, Canada, if he went there at an appointed time, he would see it in person. He did bother to go and witnessed this.

"Several years ago, flying saucer lecturer/author Orfeo Angelucci, in his book, *Secret of the Saucers*, warned of a coming 'GREAT ACCIDENT,' as given him by Space Intelligence. Serious thinkers should consider, is that 'ACCIDENT' approaching?

Getting My Act Together

The first of the books was a thrilling adventure to one just getting underway in a mission yet veiled. I awakened suddenly from a deep sleep, sat up and found myself saying the title out loud, "*World Messages For the Coming Decade.*" Well, what is it? What does it mean? Kuthumi spoke and explained I would do this little book for him and that he would supervise all of its contents. "How will you do that?" He said he would organize a list of speakers. That was one of the most amazing things to me. After telling me where I should locate myself to receive them, he gave me a list of the speakers and the times of day to expect them. There were very structured instructions concerning eating, showering, sleeping and the appointments. There were 27 speakers crowded into the seven days of vigil at Elephant Butte Lake, a lovely setting in central New Mexico. I was instructed to greet all of the elementals surrounding the cottage, to talk to the big tree in front and explain why I was there and to seek their help and protection. "The area is gentle and peaceful and conducive to your work."

Concerning end time events, the messages were of a preparatory nature. Around the same point in time, in the room where I meditated three times a day, I learned from Joshua speaking through Lucy Colson that:

"There is a beam, a vortex of energy beaming down from the heavens. The energy has specks of yellow in it, as dust particles that glisten when sun rays hit them. There is a padding or insulation where the beam hits the ceiling of the trailer, so as not to interfere with the molecules of the physical trailer. If this were not done, during a special burst of energy ray, your trailer would disintegrate, and then reappear moments later."

When I learned about the beam, I wanted to put a chair directly under it, but I was never permitted to do it as long as I lived in that trailer. That first crude edition from a totally inexperienced publisher, was filled with evidence of my ineptitude as a typist, yet, incredulously to me, souls cared enough for its messages to continue to buy it. Then an angel called Brenda Payne came into my life, and voluntarily undertook to clean up the manuscript and make it presentable, adorning it with professionalism. Her touch was important in the books that followed as well, led by God to share in the work.

I emptied all of my savings into the releasing of Kuthumi's little Golden Book and the launching of *Guardian Action Publications*. His book is now in its eighth edition, with 10,000 copies circulated. Now, years later, it is still a favorite with people, and I am glad that I told this Great Master that night, "I will do it," though I trembled within at the thought.

The first book offered a diluted explanation of the confederation, the Ashtar Command, and the part the Etheric Craft would play in end times events. A digestible approach to the Commands upon which later releases would build. I learned later the sequence of the books were all specifically planned long before the books were manifested.

ON EARTH ASSIGNMENT: THE COSMIC AWAKENING OF LIGHT WORKERS, WALK-INS AND ALL STAR-BORN REPRESENTATTIVES

The sudden commission from Commander Ashtar led to the call two years later to compile *Project World Evacuation*. There was no questioning the explicit instructions, directives were clear and the time schedule given. The setting was my quiet old farm property at the edge of Deming, New Mexico. I had learned a lot more about the book business. Immediately, the volume of mail was pleasantly overwhelming; and many study groups began to form around the volume. Returning from the Reno Convention in November, in my times of stillness, guidelines were beginning to surface for another book. Its title again was furnished from a Mother Craft and I was permitted to see the cover. The Evacuation book has had eight printings as these words are written, with 14,000 copies in circulation. It set off a controversy of vast proportions, but that was Ashtar's problem, not mine. He later released this statement in his Universal Network, quarterly journal, which came two years later:

"Hundreds upon hundreds have been secured in the Light since the publishing of the Evacuation book. Much understanding has settled in minds that were divided and unsettled. Definite positions have been taken and opened to communication and guidance. Within the last 24 months, many leaders and Commanders have been awakened to the ranks. The desired awakening has taken place and when the thrust of events is upon the world, there will be many more to assist and partake of the removal.

"Believe that within this book, we have shared all that we possibly could ... have been given that which could be given. The purpose for the revelation is directly tied to the Divine Program. Now we are watching the growth of the seed in minds and in the hearts of those who have read. As we have monitored reactions, we have learned much of the nature of hostility to it, the extent of disbelief, but primarily, the overwhelming state of readiness, of those who have grown from it."

At this point, I sensed and felt something placed in my arms, ethereally speaking. I perceived its shape and substance to be a rolled up scroll. As I realized its presence, it seemed to be growing in my arms.

"We have placed a scroll in your hands. It is given in your keeping, for upon it are the names of everyone who will be lifted up. Let the names be ethereally absorbed in your Being. Write upon your heart the names of the Children of Light, the sons and the daughters of God."

ON EARTH ASSIGNMENT: THE COSMIC AWAKENING OF LIGHT WORKERS, WALK-INS AND ALL STAR-BORN REPRESENTATTIVES

As I listened, the scroll continued to enlarge.

"Yes, there will be many more than anticipated. Many names will be added to the scroll because of our book that has gone forth. We wanted you to perceive and understand this mission of the manuscript. It was a call to prepare hearts for events, that there would be no fear, that there would be no surprise, that there would be a preparation, that there would be calls rising from the planet, on behalf of these great things that must happen. And because of the energy that will go into and has gone into those calls, it will be easier for us to perform our task, to bring the Evacuation to conclusion swiftly and smoothly."

It had been a bit difficult to understand when the Commander told me that I had spent 25 lifetimes preparing for this mission. He explained that putting the words of Ashtar before the world and the work of the Ashtar Command, would consummate my destiny.

"It was only for your service within the Intergalactic Legion of Special Volunteers, in that capacity, that I was willing to surrender you out of the Fleet as one of my chosen Commanders. I have trusted you with much and you have not disappointed me nor our Beloved Commander in Chief."

The Divine Program for Earth has ever involved this building of a bridge of trust over the waters of negativism down through the civilizations. An interesting paragraph from the Elders informs us:

"In times past, there has been a tendency on the part of people of earth to have a small wave of enthusiastic response to the messages from higher realms, and then after a brief time, to slip into a period of lethargy once more, or worse-criticism and foolishness. However, we have also noticed that, whenever these fluctuations take place on each departure from enthusiasm or interest, there are a greater number who remain steadfast. Thus, over the centuries, the number of those who are anchored in the understanding of these things has slowly increased here; quality and not quantity is the criteria. Upon this foundation of trust and understanding of a firm minority we have built our relationship with the planet."

There is no question that a much greater minority, with an understanding of the presence and the purpose of these friends from other

ON EARTH ASSIGNMENT: THE COSMIC AWAKENING OF
LIGHT WORKERS, WALK-INS AND ALL STAR-BORN REPRESENTATTIVES

worlds, is reasonably understood by a broader segment of humanity. They had kept me in waiting for over 12 years, continually admonishing that the time was not yet right. Then, suddenly, in 1980, it was time to launch their campaign.

They became enthusiastic about releasing a manuscript that would simplify an understanding of cosmic telepathy. They sensed a time in future events when individual contact could save lives. Thus they commissioned the book, *The Dynamics of Cosmic Telepathy*. All of us worked hard on it. The manuscript moved slowly. It's preparation, according to my standards, required many hours of library research, personal study, and endless appointments with Them, months on end. The book was in actual preparation for a year and I wearied with the task, but I knew that I had given it "my best shot," and had invested all I had to give of my energies and abilities. My fellow Officers of our Command were delighted with our resulting effort.

They insisted that now the time was right for such a volume, also that the many souls triggered to awakening by the other books would have simple directives to assist them."

By using simple diagrams and elementary terminology, the book was released to present a "horse sense" approach to a subject hitherto clothed in superstition and ignorance. Because of its suggestive text book format, hundreds of groups registered with us as using it for their text. Though in the past, its four editions have placed 6,000 copies, it has now taken on a new life in its going forth. This suggests a deepening of human application to the quest for expansion and understanding. It represents a resulting action our Space Friends have waited for.

The book of *Ashtar*, my tribute to my leader, was a natural outgrowth of the others as people became more and more interested in him as a person, and also as errors in concept of his Being surfaced. It was, of course, a joy to accomplish this task and a true labor of Love. The popularity of his book was astounding and gratifying on all dimensions. It accomplished much in bridging the gap between the Spiritual Hierarchy and the "flying wing" portion of the Great White Brotherhood of Light. Someone needed to accomplish this, there was too much polarizing of separateness between the Confederation, the Federation and the Celestial Groups. There was even a pronounced intolerance between physical contactees and spiritual

ON EARTH ASSIGNMENT: THE COSMIC AWAKENING OF
LIGHT WORKERS, WALK-INS AND ALL STAR-BORN REPRESENTATTIVES

contactees, a situation that brought much sadness to the Command, for we were sabotaging our own Divine Program. A heating of this rift was a strong encodenrent in my mission. I have done what I could. Commander Korton, communication coordinator, speaks to the problem:

"Basically, Light Workers must endeavor to appreciate the unified effort of the entire spiritual program for the planet, as one harmonious pictures with Universal overtones of cooperation and unity. WE ARE ALL ONE, in whatever dimension our contacts originate, and in your dimension also. WE are all laborers together in the great Divine Program ... a program designed by the Brotherhood of Light of this Universal sector, to prepare Earth to move along with its solar system into a higher frequency of spiritual awareness; specifically, to fulfill its ordained expression in a New Age, manifesting in that cycle, life on the highest plane.

"There is no place for competitiveness nor self-seeking within the ranks of Light. There can be no human element to distort those Light energies. The Program for Earth is propelled by Love and Harmony and Unity of all of its parts, and those opposing or obstructing the standard will be removed from the program!

"Many great Masters of the higher realms and many highest sources within the Galactic Commands have founded various interpretations of the Program through their chosen and proven earth representatives. One may sometimes suffer a measure of confusion with the various terminologies or system of presentation, or defaults of approach of structured methods. However, never ... I say, never... must one lay aside the vision to understand and appreciate that each various movement, small or large, though admittedly stamped with the identifying structure of its individual founder, is nevertheless but one of the working parts of the Great Body of Light in heaven and on earth. We must keep a stalwart and blanketing vision of the Big Picture, or the big umbrella of the Divine Program, overshadowing all efforts that comprise the total input of Divine Light upon the planetary scene.

"This is our deep concern at this time. Where there has been division ... polarizing, paralyzing, chemicalizations ... of a certain way, a preferred method, a chosen approach, these have been within the human scope of free will chosen approach, these have been within the human scope of free will choice, as individuals sought their preferred pathway. Never must that preferred pathway be exalted above others, or used to Lord one's choice over the choice of another. Rather, realize that all men are, at some point, upon the Pathway, and they are where they are, primarily because that is where it is best for them to be at this point in their personal development and enlightenment. So be ye not judging not intolerant of one another, but give space to all souls to expand in their chosen manner, their chosen pace, and their chosen methodology, realizing that at this moment in the Program, Light has increased a hundredfold, within access of all humanity for its spiritual needs.

"As Guardians and Watchmen of this unfoldment, we render assistance to souls in whatever Pathway they have chosen, knowing that choice is subject to constant change as growth continues unhindered. Love the Christed Image within all, understanding that Light upon any Pathway is a moving, living force producing continuing viable change in that lifestream. As individuals expectant of that change, hold your 'sacred cows' loosely at all times, ready for sudden guidance into new understanding and experience. Keep your minds open, to consider and discern all things; neither to reject nor accept, but to hold in your consciousness until clearer understanding follows. Hold your hearts open to accept all who conscientiously seek wisdom, in their fashion. The love of the Guardians is ever with you. I am Korton, your communications coordinator within the solar system."

By this time, the shipping needs and related correspondence of *Guardian Action* had grown to demanding proportions, and my Space Friends lifted up their eyes unto a field white for harvest. The progress report on people in general who had now acquired and followed their words, reflected great growth in understanding and it was determined that a different type of material, more learned and involved, could be shared with them. "We want to find out where the mighty ones are!" Therefore, they launched their own quarterly journal, Universal Network, which represented a network of speakers from the Universe.

"The response to your heavier type of newsletter has been very pleasing to us, and we have used it as a finding device, so to speak, in discerning the depth of many. It is designed for those who are beyond the neophyte stage, to nourish their desire for strong meat. Amongst the few that matter, the general understanding of our nature, mission and purpose is fairly well digested and applied."

ON EARTH ASSIGNMENT: THE COSMIC AWAKENING OF LIGHT WORKERS, WALK-INS AND ALL STAR-BORN REPRESENTATTIVES

It was generally agreed that, within the mystical number of three, the newsletter would run for three years and complete a mystical number of 12; we almost made it, didn't we? We had to cease operation after the tenth issue and two and a half years of effort, but Universal Network certainly did have its "day in the sun" with incredulous popularity and support. Earthly circumstances intervened as they often do, and we were released from the commitment a bit early.

In the meantime, I had been in touch with Ruth Montgomery by letter, by phone. In one of her letters, she wrote:

"I asked the 'guides' about you and they wrote: Tuella is a being from outer space. There is indeed an Ashtar Command guarding Earth to rescue those worthy ones who will contribute to rejuvenation of Earth after the Shift, when they will return. Including outer space volunteers here to help others accommodate to changing times, to prevent war, to prepare for inevitability of the Shift. Take seriously what Tuella reports."

-Ruth Montgomery

Because of this, she graciously mentioned our work in her newest book, *Aliens Among Us*. This gesture produced a swelling in our mailing list of incredible response. The interaction between the Special Earth Volunteers has a wonderful way of coming to pass and helping one another. The obedient Volunteer, walking steadfastly in the Light of his own Mission, can almost just stand back and behold the handiwork of God in his or her life. The Divine Program is the greatest commitment we can make during our embodiment.

The work of Light is not just a Sunday stroll. It is a constant application of your best effort. It is taking dominion. It is obtaining the promises, it is ... warfare. If need be, you go til you drop. I did!

It had been my custom to cram three long lectures and rap sessions into one day at the seminars, so that folks wouldn't have so much expense for meals and motels, or a long, exhausting attendance at the activity. The next day, I would feel like an empty feed sack to hang on a nail or collapse in a pile on the floor. These intensives took the last drop of energy I had to give and spread it amongst the people to take home with them. This they did and it made a difference everywhere. So many of them are out there now in the field serving the Program of Light in their own intensive way.

ON EARTH ASSIGNMENT: THE COSMIC AWAKENING OF LIGHT WORKERS, WALK-INS AND ALL STAR-BORN REPRESENTATTIVES

The last year of that kind of service, I totally used all of the reserve and beyond it; the three seminars of 1985 at Anaheim, Albuquerque and Honolulu did me in. It took a year and a half to physically bounce back, but bounce I did.

A totally new experience came out of the Anaheim Seminar in the unexpected, unprepared for, production of a four-hour video album. This certainly was not my intention. It just seemed to be an idea whose time had come and others furnished the momentum, the expertise, and organization for it. What seemed to be the last lectures I would be able to share with people have since gone out everywhere, in all directions, to souls who would never have attended in person. A wonderful new tool for the Light Workers of the planet. With my trophy of the master video tapes in my suitcase, I came home to enter an exciting new field-video producer. I personally designed the color wrapper, edited the tape and launched an ongoing distribution. Truly you are never too old to learn something new.

Like the new kid on the block, a new file on my desk was getting a lot of attention. My Space Friends and I jokingly labeled it, "*Tuella and the ET's.*" It was the seed of this manuscript. They were planning it even then. Ashtar and Lord Sananda insisted that people would be inspired by such a record, but I remained hard to convince, lacking enthusiasm. Nevertheless, I continued to feed the file with dictations and scraps of paper, until a long period of illness and recuperation efforts pushed it from my mind.

When physical strength and zest for life returned, Ashtar reopened the channel and presented a new task very close to his heart. He wanted us to jointly create a movie script to reach several million people in one tremendous effort. He contributed specific guidelines and much input. He is now seeking a financial benefactor into whose hands he will place the money to be given. I contended that they were no longer producing epics and collossals, but he maintains that, through the Ashtar Command, this one WILL be produced. What an unexcelled method for reaching the masses with his message! The movie script was completed before Harmonic Convergence was upon us. With a burst of enthusiasm, coupled with a regret for the long delay, I had begun serious work on this manuscript. And then the sun rose on August 17, 1987—Ashtar had other plans!

ON EARTH ASSIGNMENT: THE COSMIC AWAKENING OF LIGHT WORKERS, WALK-INS AND ALL STAR-BORN REPRESENTATTIVES

The Decodernent of Vegan

The first few days just prior to the Harmonic Convergence we had been guiding by telephone the meditation efforts of a soul brother some distance away. On August 17th, he experienced his own memory cells explosion, beginning a period of decodement and revelation he could scarcely handle.

The first few days were devastating in their inroads within the body, mind, and spirit of VEGAN as the revelation was faced, accepted, and gradually understood. We gave him much assistance and guidance at that tender time. When the week had passed, ASHTAR'S SON was beautifully established and grown in stature; notably his ability to counsel, visibly, with those of the highest dimensions. With deep incredulity, he learned of his heritage. He learned his father is the most powerful and well known of all the Commanders of the entire Extraterrestrial Commands and leader of the universally represented ASHTAR COMMAND. His father is my old friend and yours, beloved COMMANDER ASHTAR.

VEGAN has full vision of those who spoke with him and is often lifted up into the etheric to meet with others. The son, VEGAN, has manifested to the planet 17 times before, and it has always been for a profound purpose.

VEGAN and I, Tuella, during that Holy Week, many times were receiving the identical messages from ASHTAR simultaneously, occasionally even while telephoning. It was explained that, in one of the early years of the '40's, seven Commanders lowered themselves into earth's atmosphere an&, for one year, experienced embodiment. Seven sons were born, one to each Commander. Vegan was told:

"My son, you are the first of the seven etherics on the planet to gain full realization, and are therefore the most vulnerable. You are of royalty, and the Son of ASHTAR. With you, VEGAN, there were two other contacts; one as a child of seven, and then again at 17 or so. It was agreed then, we would return to you at this Holy Time of Harmonic Convergence, but that conversation was blocked from your memory until August 18, 1987, at which time it has been repeated again. The remaining six etheric sons of Commanders, not yet unveiled, are now in Great Britain, Peru, Canada, southwest Asia, Australia and northern France; each of different fathers, but all sons of Commanders."

A few years beyond the teenage encounter, there began to develop upon the right palm of VEGAN, the six-pointed (double triangle) star with a "V" and a dot in its center; the sign which his Commander father identified as being the seal of VEGAN the prophet. The star is now very prominent upon his palm.

VEGAN not only knows immediately of the presence of any dark Princes of the dark realms, but also knows their status and their names and titles. They have a fear of him and tremendous efforts will be made to seek and to destroy him, but to no avail. VEGAN was told that ANTON would come to herald his revelation and pay his respects. His great craft came, and for three days and nights it hung visibly at the edge of the small village where all could see it, while ANTON visited with him as well as other Command dignitaries. Original copies of VEGAN'S signed and documented transmissions from his father, ASHTAR, are secured by *GUARDIAN ACTION INTERNATIONAL.*

We here, of course, have always known that GUARDIAN ACTION unit has always been dear to ASHTAR'S heart, but the things he spoke to his son were "mind-blowing" to us also. The commander told VEGAN he is particularly an etheric guard and protector of "our Tuella," and even though far separated from her physically speaking, knows immediately the very moment when she is threatened in any way. ASHTAR instructed VEGAN, his son:

"Work diligently with 'our Tuella' and *Guardian Action International*. They, only, have exclusive release of any of VEGAN'S material. The Great Councils were unanimous in their approval of her to handle this great, responsibility. She is well equipped in her unveiling and intellect to handle this development. She is a strong, loved, and respected member of our Family. We will be grateful to her for many lifetimes to come. She is like a Cosmic Mother to all of us here; respect her and listen to her counsel."

ASHTAR repeatedly monitored our telephone conversations and often interrupted with helpful information which we both heard. We prepared a notarized document officially appointing VEGAN as Ambassador-at-large for Guardian Action International, and our association in joint

ON EARTH ASSIGNMENT: THE COSMIC AWAKENING OF
LIGHT WORKERS, WALK-INS AND ALL STAR-BORN REPRESENTATTIVES

service to the planet was launched.

From the onset of his experience, VEGAN was instructed to contact Tuella with all his information for her help continually:

"It is Tuella's responsibility to alert all of earth's Volunteers of the presence of ASHTAR'S son. Tuella is our trusted messenger of Light. She has known you, VEGAN, for many lifetimes. In the etheric she has been your trusted friend and teacher. She will continue to guide, and I trust her with your learning completely. She has been chosen from all of the Volunteers upon the planet for this task, and she has always brought us honor."

On August 24, 1987, Commander ASHTAR dictated to VEGAN and signed this DECREE:

"I, ASHTAR, decree *GUARDIAN ACTION INTERNATIONAL* as my official clearinghouse; the proper home for my son's information and influence to center around the world. I continue to channel through others, but I pronounce this UNIT and TUELLA as my official Earth Base. This is decreed the 24th day of August, 1987 earth years. I AM ASHTAR, Father of VEGAN."

This tremendous convergence of unveiling reached its climax at the important PISCES full moon September 7. We at GUARDIAN ACTION INTERNATIONAL met in joint meditation with VEGAN. ASHTAR took his turn of blessing all of us in a magnificent way. It was at this PISCES hour of closeness to the etheric that VEGAN totally entered into and completed his full initiation; solemnly taking his vows to follow a life similar to that of Jesus the Christ, as well as his solemn vow of celibacy.

On that night, VEGAN wrote:

"I stood in the trees surrounded by the sounds of the night. The full moon illuminated my surroundings. Suddenly, at precisely 10:00 PM, the scene took oil a much more intense glow. I tingled from head to toe and felt my Father approaching me. I turned and faced him IN THE FLESH AND BLOOD! His silver suit shimmered in the glow. The long blond hair combed back to his shoulder, and those incredible eyes! My breath caught in my throat and he smiled. His hand extended toward me, and I reached for it. Our hands clasped and he drew near. We embraced as father to son, and the feelings that rushed from his being to mine nearly caused me to col-

ON EARTH ASSIGNMENT: THE COSMIC AWAKENING OF LIGHT WORKERS, WALK-INS AND ALL STAR-BORN REPRESENTATTIVES

lapse. I wept. I felt electrically charged. We parted and took seven steps back. I spotted a tear in his eye. He gestured for me to kneel, and I obeyed, as the exchanges involved in my initiation and vows began. My head remained bowed throughout. When I was finally permitted to raise my gaze, I saw dear Monka in glowing silver, at my father's right hand, and very dashing Andromeda to his left, with his combed back jet black hair and intriguing green eyes sparkling in the moonlight.

There were two distinct gusts of wind from two opposite directions; one from the east, one from the west. On this clear night, there was a flash of what appeared as lightning and a loud crack of thunder. They were gone, and I stood alone as I had come. When I returned to the car, my friend who stood guard had taken notes and verified the intense glow, like a dome. He had also written of the weird lightning and thunder, of several shooting stars and an orange 'ball' overhead. When I entered the car, the lights and windshield wipers came on, and my friend almost freaked out. I calmed him by laughing. We saw frost and small pieces of ice on my eyebrows and hair. My body was icy, but there was a warmness in my being that remained for over 12 hours. IT WAS A MAGNIFICENT INITIATION!"

This, then, was the completion of the Revelation. Because of the scope and breadth of the commission to "alert all earth volunteers," Commander Ashtar changed the name of the earthbased unit to *Guardian Action International*. Our first step was a personal letter of report to about 50 prominent international leaders encoded with the frequency of the Ashtar Command, in advance of the general announcement.

The book manuscript was laid aside, and a proposed tour of Australia cancelled, as we plunged into the effort to rally the forces of Light and mobilize their strength. This new commission of Ashtar flooded our hearts. We knew we must accelerate activities and expand the Divine Plan to fruition. Our inadequate office and staff became a feverish beehive of labors to be worthy of Ashtar's honored assignment. Our mailing list could touch about 8,000 interested souls, who could in turn touch others. So many of these loving ones had stood loyally beside us in crisis after crisis, and, again, we knew the Commander could count on the energies of their faithfulness to assist and join us. Like autumn leaves swept into sudden motion by a whirling gust of wind, lethargy vanished and action became the order of the day. The fervor of the response gladdened his heart.

**ON EARTH ASSIGNMENT: THE COSMIC AWAKENING OF
LIGHT WORKERS, WALK-INS AND ALL STAR-BORN REPRESENTATTIVES**

We were asked to "build a Golden Circle" of souls who would affiliate themselves openly and fearlessly with the Ashtar Command. To do this, we had to computerize our efficiency, magnetize volunteer help and manifest adequate headquarters. It was an exciting time! Lord Ashtar had also ordained that Guardian Action International sponsor Vegan's counseling ministry by mail. A willing group typed the 8,000 labels, and local volunteers expedited several bulk mailings. Every need was met and a new publication, The Golden Circle, was launched. Several thousand souls were quickened within to remember the Divine Program and their part in it.

The obedient Volunteer, walking steadfastly in the Light of their own assignment, can stand aside and behold the handiwork of God in their life. The Divine Program is decidedly the greatest commitment we can make during our embodiment on earth.

Life's Highest Purpose

Divine Will

Chapter 3

Surrender

The Crucifixion of Jesus the Christ, Our Lord Sananda, is symbolical of what all Overcomers must face in this embodiment. He knew Himself to be the One who had come to take upon Himself a part of the Karma of the world, so that man would not be crushed by his own Karma and miss his opportunity on this platform of evolution. The load was so heavy Terra itself reeled to and fro. Mankind could not have found his way to Truth and Light. So this Great Cosmic Being, once again, laid aside His Splendor to walk this Pathway, in His Purity, His Majesty, and take upon Himself a portion of that Karma. No man could take His life from Him, He stated, "I LAY IT DOWN..." Dark forces were permitted to touch that body, that all who come after would be able to make their Ascension, if they willed to do so.

Our Beloved Lord Michael, Archangel of the Angel Kingdom and Angels of the Blue Ray, spoke to me long ago:

"Heaven awaits the disciple who ponders these truths. Without this wisdom, no initiate has ever advanced upon the Path. And the Masters who lead them, must wait in the shadows for their chela to evolve into wisdom. Your life in this incarnation has unfolded much because of your soul ability to handle chastenings during your progressing evolution. You have made the crossing safely. You have entered the hall of learning and your studies have begun. Step by step, we will lead you into greater initiations, serving others as you go along; but the supreme ecstasy of your Being will be your entering into the deeper Initiations through which your Master will lead you.

"You cannot walk these paths alone, for only in Our Guidance and Support could you find your way. We call all chelas to lay aside human ego, human goals or human boastfulness, to enter into that Crucifixion of the Lower Self that brings the glorious resurrection of the Christ Spirit within. Let the Bright Angel within destroy the Tomb itself, and rise in Newness of Life. I AM MICHAEL. I stand before your soul as you walk through these gates of learning and I close these gates behind you. I am your Fiery Guardsman in action."

In *The Gentle Brother*, White Eagle has written:

May the rose boom upon your cross. Interpreted, this means, may you through constant striving towards the Light, transmute the heaviness of the cross of matter into the fragrant rose of the spiritual life."

In the mystic teachings of crucifixion and resurrection, the descent of the spirit of man into matter is the outcome of the need for purification and regeneration. To live in such a manner of overcoming and retracing old steps, to return reborn again into yet a higher state of being, reveals that life itself is crucifixion in the flesh. The whole meaning and mystery of the Truth we love is the magical process of transformation and transmutation. For the earthbased volunteer on the cross of embodiment, enduring purification is also, at the same time, transforming and transmuting everything surrounding us as well. Every ordeal endured is not only changing us, but the environment around us. One embodiment is but a footstep in the sands of time.

The Cross, as a symbol, was used thousands of years before the Christian Era. It appeared on the temple walls and on the Obelisks of Egypt, with an emblem of a flower in the center. It symbolized the Embodiment of Man with the center flower representing the unfolding of the soul. Evolving, growing through the tests, the trials, the endurance of human life experiences. It was a philosophical symbol of embodied sons and daughters of God nailed to the cross of karma for this platform of evolution. The Great Law picks on no man, has no favorites, is no respecter of persons. The Law of Cause and Effect is totally impersonal, in that whatever is sown is reaped, somehow, sometime, somewhere. Perhaps the man on the street can rebel against his karma, but a disciple can only obey and endure with-

ON EARTH ASSIGNMENT: THE COSMIC AWAKENING OF
LIGHT WORKERS, WALK-INS AND ALL STAR-BORN REPRESENTATTIVES

out a murmur and it is the quality of that obedience that measures the integrity of the Volunteer.

Birth is a doorway. The door opens and we enter. Think of all that must be left behind on the other side of the door. The Vision, the glory, the lovely etheric body, the beautiful remains, the total spiritual awareness, akashic awareness, the records and memories. Now the body chemical must be taken up. After all those beautiful high vibrations, now the entity must slow down to a crawl. The physical body must be fed, housed, clothed, taken care of, trained, protected, educated. Slipping into all of these limitations from a place of unlimited space and freedom, we then spend the rest of the incarnation becoming an overcomer of these limitations. Every limitation of embodiment becomes a challenge that can be overcome when all limitations are lifted to spiritual levels; when physical purpose becomes one in unity and purpose with the spirit oversoul. One by one the shackles and chains of limitations of embodiment drop off as the soul finds freedom again!

The whole meaning of transformation is attainment through initiation. Attainment is not:
- being learned in outputs of revelation
- how many years spent in structured classes -rudeness
- an argumentative spirit
- terminology hair splitting
- spiritual tantrums when karma must descend
- talking to the Masters

Attainment is:
- Mastery itself
- the grace to follow
- the grace to cooperate
- never giving or causing hurt to another
- courtesy
- tolerance
- strength in quietness
- serenity
- mastery of the emotional body
- mastery of the mental body
- mastery of the physical body
- forbearance, long-suffering
- patience and endurance.

ON EARTH ASSIGNMENT: THE COSMIC AWAKENING OF
LIGHT WORKERS, WALK-INS AND ALL STAR-BORN REPRESENTATTIVES

It is the Mastery of Love in Action, but it comes through human Initiation on the cross of crucifixion of self wants, self plans, self desires, self ambitions. When self is slain, the resurrection of Spirit that follows transmutes everything around it.

Yield not to the temptation of self-preservation. Shut out the voices that clamor for one to "come down off the cross, if you be God." In that moment of seeming helplessness, totally victimized by prevailing circumstances, the Beloved who could have called Legions of Angels to His rescue, remained to accomplish more for the world in that one moment of time than any other had ever done. The Earth Based volunteer will also be reviled by the cry, "If you be a child of God, then why is this happening to you?" Answer them not, in quietness is your strength. Within the inner citadel, be still and know that your Father hath not forsaken you. Frederick Von Mierers has captured the truth of the Spiritual resurrection in these words:

"The material world is symbolized by the cross, the two great beams of time an space, upon which everything in the visible world must be crucified in order to achieve resurrection. All things visible return to the All-Invisible. Where these beams cross and meet is the here and now; the only place where matter exists at all.

"The Divine Self, the I AM of you, must be crucified as well upon the cross in matter, in order to achieve resurrection into the Eternal Reality within. To become enlightened, or divinely magnetized, you must conquer your lower subject-object self by crucifying it on the beams of time and space-the cross. Only by suffering, which is a crucifixion, will you be able to overcome the personal ego.

"Through your suffering, you begin to look for a solution, a solution existing within yourself, your Higher Self, the I AM of you. This is the true meaning of the Resurrection. You rise from LIMITED body consciousness into the unlimited awareness of the Eternal Reality which animates you and every living creature."

The self nature or outer mind is the carnal covering of the inner splendor. In the brush with outward test and trials, one needs only to extravagantly let go of one's lower fears, lower opinions, lower reactions, returning the gift of free-will back to Him who gave it. It is here that desirelessness becomes a status of the inner being. Then and only then is the true death to ignorance (which is darkness) and the awakening unto the law written within the human heart. Thus we become bondslaves of Love, and not bondslaves of law. Ashtar explains:

"The principle of free will is not necessary in our worlds because every man desires only the will of the Father, the Radiant One. We have no other will; the reign of Self Will no longer exists. This is the secret of the dark effluvia that surrounds the Earth. This is the cause for its need of cleansing. Allowing the will of God in emotions, thoughts and feeling world; in deed and action; in every spoken word. This is the underlying principle of all Universal Law. We have always admired the simplicity of the query, "What would Jesus do?" "What would a Master do in this situation in which I FIND MYSELF? If I allow my Christed self to handle this problem, what would be done?" Meditation such as this, in the unpleasant moments of life, being Light and change to the world in general and the personal world in particular."

Vortex Points and the Memory Veil

Reverend Hal Wilcox is an outstanding contactee of the fifties, remaining continuously active in interplanetary affairs as representative of the planet Alpha Centauri. He has a fascinating teaching concerning The Memory Veil, and we quote his material here:

"What are now called vortex points in our words were at one time Space Marker Buoys placed on our planet's grid system. This Galaxy was explored and those 49 planets which could support human life were marked with Buoys so they could be watched and handled like a garden, as described in the first pages of our Holy Bible.

"The seven days of creation describe how a virgin galaxy or planet was gradually molded, step by step, until simple forms of life were observed to survive, by way of Space Markers, each capable of transceiving (both directions) all data. The planets and the 'Watchers' (buoys) are connected until the entire Galaxy became a realistic TEST STATION. The test was/is to develop a method by which mankind throughout the entire universe could live in peace under God as one United Government.

"Their locations are exact, so that the transmitted energy can power them, which is called Shel Force in the E.T. language. Stones of granite absorb this force, God's power of Life, much as a stone absorbs heat in the desert sun. All these six fixed computer devices are located on the exact strongest vortex points man has evolved, along with other life forms, around them.

"Each century, man understood these structures better, until eventually he began to develop to a point that we/he could understand two basic things; communication and transportation. With these concepts, mankind on earth was ready to grasp the difference between rock structures (Gizeh, Stonehenge, Chichen-Itza, etc.) and a Terminal Computer. At that point, people on each of the 49 planets colonized, were able to understand that these terminals were important. These notions did not include the wisdom, understanding or experience regarding terminal computers, so man hadn't the foggiest idea why certain places, temples, or objects were important.

"Atlantis (Lemuria), and Antilla were but two civilizations on our planet that completed all of the cultural exchange projects with E.T. communication. Yet every one of our past civilizations has failed the test, due to the lack of development and experience, much as on the other 48 colonized planets. These people also went through a similar struggle.

There was a major difference between the end of the failure of Atlantis and that of Antilla, in that our planet was completely 'washed clean' at the end of the first civilization mentioned. This created a large gap of time until man was again able to inhabit this earth as a 'dwelling place.' With Antilla, only the human memories were 'wiped clean.' These memory devices had, from the first colonizations, been used to restore the individual soul memory of mankind. Restoring the soul meant to re-record all of the learned experiences of all past lives (that are stored in crystals) into the memory of the physical brain.

"The word Atlantis is an ET word which means God's Domain, yet it is more of a status report of a civilization, such as: 'America's destiny is to be the Atlantis reborn. There were two major land bodies, one called Atlantis and the other, Lemuria, which tends to confuse the more important concept: Both were part of the one civilization called Atlantis.'

"When God's Dwelling Place (Atlantis) became corrupted, the

physical land (like a chemical test tube) required a complete "washing" before it could be used again. This according to God's act, or to put it another way, according to Divine Principles of the Universe. Only after our planet earth was "washed clean" did those ETs who now help us, 're-seed' the human population of our 'washed world,' requiring some 250,000 years.

"The next civilization was known as Antilla, which also failed. According to God's promises, symbolized by the rainbow, our planet and those people of Antilla did not suffer another total earth wash. Instead, the world was 'wiped clean' by the power of the Energy of Babel. There was a Tower of Babel, which made it possible for complete interface between Universal Mind and the individual terminal brain/body and the citizens of Antilla. Babel was also the name of the wireless computer link between our earth in Mighty Gizeh, to the network of computers and all the United Worlds. This included all those planets (and other dwelling places, ships, stations, etc.) which had successfully 'graduated.'

"Knowing that 'The Two' had brought about another planetary failure in Antilla, all the devices were removed from Gizeh and hidden. Afterwards, the mercy of our Common Creator intervened and allowed for a small group, the GWB, to retain their memories. However, instead of 'washing the planet' again, TOTAL MEMORY WAS REMOVED FROM THE PLANET EARTH, a condition which still is in effect.

"There has been a, span of some 25,000 years from the event, during which 'the memory veil' was lowered, until the date known to us as February 5, 1962 ... also called THE NEW AGE. It requires a great deal of thought to grasp the importance and significance of the statement, 'All memory has been removed from planet earth.' We are now in that state of mental awareness today, and although the word 'memory' is in our vocabulary, we do not know the true and correct meaning of such a statement as it applies to our Spiritual Being. All memories of all lives is not the same concept as all memories of one life. In fact, this only opens a crack in the door to a fuller meaning: All memory of all Knowledge in the Universe, or Superconsciousness.

"Those who 'graduate' will have their total Soul Memory restored, along with an open awareness to all knowledge. The 23rd Psalm hits the nail right on the head by saying: He restores my soul. Restoring the soul = restoring soul memory, which means returning something that was taken away, as in the sentence: 'All memory was removed from the people of earth.

"Our Elder Brothers came to help guide the Egyptian Mystery Schools. The memory device maintained a continuous flow of awareness, communication or memory for Nefertiti and her Egyptian Mystery Schools. The stories of Nefertiti and her Oracles have been passed down to us as Ayesha, She, etc. in legend and verse, becoming the basis for our present World Religions.

"Not knowing what these Soul Restoring Devices were, the people of each century tended those empty cradles for the Ino Computers. They like past earth humans, placed flowers on these Temples of Consciousness ... like graves. And like graves, we fell into the practice of placing dead bodies into containers to be worshiped, while the Soul of Man was thrown out and considered worthless! As the human re-seeding continued these past 25,000 years, women bore the seed of The Universal Race, from these temples of ancient learning ... just as selected men were giving guiding Wisdom. The stories told were much like that of Moses, who spoke through a Terminal Device on the Holy Mountain. It is not an accident that much of the Holy Bible contains the Original 12 Commandments, given as the laws of God's Covenant through a Burning Bush."

As I studiously considered the above article again, I was reminded of a message received from Joshua, Lucy Colson's Master, when he spoke concerning my Notre Dame Cathedral experience on a visit to Paris:

"You were sent there for realignment purposes. While you sat in the Cathedral and communed in your physical form, the emotional body was being strengthened and aligned for that which lay ahead for you. It was a necessary trip, for you needed the extra jolt of spiritual energy to charge your finer bodies, to make the realignment stick. Your extremely weak 'signal' made the readjustment very hard to make and it would not have taken hold had you been anywhere else. For as you sat upon that very spot, under the Cathedral ran lines of magnetic energy coursing through the earth, which acted as a grounding device. They also acted in a magnetic way of drawing off the negative energies out of your feet, as more and more of the Divine energies were filtered through to your spiritual body, and then down into the physical, until you were completely cleansed. You were put into a "holding pattern" there and nothing else interested you because all your senses

ON EARTH ASSIGNMENT: THE COSMIC AWAKENING OF LIGHT WORKERS, WALK-INS AND ALL STAR-BORN REPRESENTATTIVES

were attuned to this one major endeavor."

A tremendous force of compulsion had intruded into my life and swept me off to Paris when I had no plans for such at all, like a force of destiny. I knew that the Cathedral was a focus for Mother Mary in Europe and went at first for that reason, but it was the great altar of Joan of Arc that drew me again and again. It was in the Cathedral that I learned of having been the mother of this great saint and I enjoyed paying homage at each of her shrines in that city. I would rise at the crack of dawn to make my daily trek to Notre Dame and have it all to myself long before the tourist buses would close in upon it. Sitting on those old hand-hewn benches and a place of prayer since the twelfth century, was indeed an experience. Then to be told that I sat in the identical spot 200 years before was a mind blower. Yes Paris was a joy to me; all the lovely Cathedrals brought such a sense of deja vu, and I had a "happy back-home-again" feeling, until I passed the Place de Concord, where once the infamous guillotine stood. As lovely as that spot is now landscaped, I could not bear to look upon it as the taxi whizzed by. An overpowering sorrow swept over me. I knew within me that one of my lives had ended upon that spot. I turned to look out the back window of the taxi and my eyes fell upon the Cathedral of Mary Magdalene. I felt a strong compulsion to go there, but did not make it. How many times, we do walk, where once we have walked before. We clue into the sorrow we have known before, or the joys, as the veil is lifted but a crack, away from our Being, only to be dropped again. But those rare moments of recall remain with us forever after.

At a certain point in the teachings of the venerated Edgar Cayce, Aura charts and Life Seals were given. These and the readings established the value and the necessity of a visual impetus for the unconscious. A personal event in my life illustrated this truth.

I am not a Catholic nor have I ever been in this current lifetime, neither have I been religiously oriented to prayer beads or visual aids to worship. Nevertheless, at a point in time, a lovely large crucifix came into my possession. As I would enter the higher state of consciousness in meditation, I found myself instinctively drawn to it and I unconsciously began to hold it against my forehead for attunement. Great floods of love would engulf me. Times when in an intensity of worship and love for the Heavenly Father, I could only seem to find relief when I would clutch the crucifix to my bosom. All of my Orthodox teaching notwithstanding, in the quietness of soul that followed, I found myself making the sign of the Cross with an emotion kindred to a parting embrace. I believe the visual impetus of the crucifix was kicking in recall form my many incarnations as a Sister behind cloistered walls in many different civilizations.

Perhaps this visual impetus explains the place of the yellow rosebud in early meditation rituals for entering the silence and established that closeness of rapport with my Invisible Friends. Paintings of the masters do this for many souls.

In the late seventies, while still in the Capital area, I had a copy of a painting called by the world *"Veronica's Handkerchief,"* or *"Veil,"* which portrays Jesus' crowned with thorns, and eyes that appear to open and close. I found at that time that, as I looked upon the thorns, it was easier to meditate upon the ideal of Spirit Self rising and conquering the earth self.

I Was There!

A heavy fog hung in the atmosphere over Washington, D.C., on Tuesday morning, March 6, 1973. Its presence pressed relentlessly into the canyons between the high rise structures. I noted at 8:00 AM that the garden apartments across from our parking area could scarcely been seen. Succumbing to a losing battle with a current virus influence, I had decided to continue to rest through my nine o'clock devotional. I turned on my right side, letting my gaze rest upon the painting of Jesus and the crown of thorns which hung beside the bed.

I do not know how much time passed, or when it began, but I became aware of the weight of great sorrow penetrating my inner being. It silently enveloped me much as spilled water might seep across a carpeted floor. It was as if the sun had set upon my life, leaving an aching eventide of despair. I sensed myself sitting upon the ground in a cross-legged position, arms folded over bosom, fingernails pressing painfully into upper arms, while the body rocked to and fro with the blurred eyes of one who does not understand. I raised my vision upward, to look upon a limp form, hanging there upon a beam and cross beam. In the manner of one beyond reasoning, I wept, "They killed Him, they killed Him. He was so beautiful, so pure, so loving, and they KILLED Him." Far away in the distance, another part of me called out futilely, "But they haven't. He is alive ... move forward to His Ascension."

ON EARTH ASSIGNMENT: THE COSMIC AWAKENING OF
LIGHT WORKERS, WALK-INS AND ALL STAR-BORN REPRESENTATTIVES

But I could not move away from the paralyzing imprisonment of memory recall of what it had been like to watch Jesus die! I genuinely tried, but the mind would not loosen its hold on the grim panorama. Dazedly, I discerned the outline of five figures ascending hurriedly up the hillside. I turned my burning swollen eyes, through the cold mist of evening fog, to more clearly see them. His Mother sat beside me, silent in her grief.

The men spread what appeared to be a soil cloth on the ground and had gathered at His feet. Three of them took a firm grasp upon the base of the middle beam, slowly raising it up and out of its pit. The others walked their hands down the back of the beam as it was gently lowered in their direction. "O my poor Lord, how thin he looks." He had been so robust but now the tall frame had such a lanky look. "O my Lord." The loin cloth that had covered Our Teacher fell to the ground. One of the men picked it up and stuffed it into his bosom with a free hand.

The men worked in silent unison, quickly completing the grim mission. I recognized the big one, but the one in the fancy cloak I had not seen before. They worked with an air of uneasiness, aware of the eyes upon them of those whom they feared. They wrapped Him well in the sail cloth. The big one carried Him down the hill and we all followed in a piercing silence; but I do not remember that walk nor the procession beyond that.

With an inner knowing, a conviction held me to the thought, that these memories had been but a prelude to the vision I then experienced. I saw His beloved head lying turned to one side, still upon the sail cloth but resting higher on a couch shaped stone. The thorns had been removed, but His hair was matted with blood from the wounds, mixed with dust from the roads. I realized the hand I saw pushing the hair from off his face was my own! In this dual role of both distant spectator and participant, I was locked into the moment with the amazement of the former and tender grief of the other. Vaguely I knew several others busied themselves around me cleansing His limbs and arms, working hurriedly, for darkness was fast closing around us. I pulled the cloth from under my shawl with which I had wiped His feet earlier in the day, as He shouldered the burden of his beams. I tenderly wiped away the grime of the day (0 Infamous Day) from that dear Face, and moistened the lips with moisture from my own. Then they were dragging me away. We hurried to leave for the guards approached and night had come.

ON EARTH ASSIGNMENT: THE COSMIC AWAKENING OF
LIGHT WORKERS, WALK-INS AND ALL STAR-BORN REPRESENTATTIVES

With this, the shattering torrents of recall had subsided and withdrawn, leaving in their wake the limp debris of a numb ache and an undertow of emptiness. I was stunned. Overcome with the reality of the scene, the sorrow of the woman, whose sorrow was indeed my own. Of this I was certain! A memory of heartache so vivid that these many lifetimes could not erase it from the soul of me. If this was what was meant by far-memory I wanted no more of it. How wise that "God in love, a veil doth throw across the way." No living human being could bear the pain of re-membering other lives with this accompanying intensity.

I touched into the emotional depth of the moment. How could I grasp the illusory idea that in a matter of hours the adeptness of His Mastership would dematerialize His body and materialize it to appear again and again and continuing again? What did I know of such things? Never again would the Loving Hand touch my head as He passed by. Those sad eyes that would sometimes meet mine for a moment of warm interchange, were closed forever. Yet that distant part of me seemed to know that at a later time I would come to understand. In the Afterwards, the guilt feelings that beset those who bury their dead, is sometimes an impenetrable haze. With all the shame of a Peter who had denied Him thrice, I was smitten with my own reproach, but simultaneously a great healing was taking place within the soul of me. In retrospect, I knew now why Good Friday and Easter Sunday had always been such times of sorrow for me. Why in the very middle of an Easter Sunday solo I would be crushed to silence with overpowering emotions. I was there! I understood why the crucifix had been such a release for me. I was there! I knew then, why in this lifetime's experiences I had gone that "second mile" again and again; turned the other cheek time after time after time; felt a fellowship with Him in His sufferings that others could not understand. Incredibly I KNEW that in every lifetime since That Day, I had served His Truth. Listlessly, I looked at the clock. It was only 8:15. 1 had relived these things in a matter of minutes!

I traced the yellow pattern of the daisies in the nylon canopy above me, another, another, and another, and another. Why had this mystical experience been given me? And, Oh my aching heart, why did it rest its revelation at so dark an hour, instead of progressing onward to its triumph. There was no joy here, what was its purpose? Where was its message?

That night, as I sat upon the couch in prayer, He came and stood before me. He made me understand the healing that had taken place in my soul records; that I would never again grieve for Him or look back upon that scene in sorrow. That its memory would be washed away, and that I was bound to Him with ties of Love that can never be broken; against which the gates of Hell cannot prevail. I had been one of the seventy who had traveled with Him. The mobs were as familiar with my face as any of the others. He said that many of them had fallen away, but I had remained faithful to the end. He confirmed that all recurring incarnations had been spent in the Father's work ... Each one had been a repetition, in Spirit, of that one.

He detailed several lifetimes as a Nun in His Name. Three times receiving renown for piety, wisdom and devotedness to His Cause. He spoke of a lifetime as a woman who healed the sick, but knew it not, for woman was subdued in her role in those times!

"But your hands were healing hands as they ministered to those who suffered. Your heart has been drawn to much exercise in prayer. We now bring you the mission of this lifetime as the greatest of them all. To become a Messenger instrument, for the closing days of time, to be expanded as the people are ready."

(I later learned that two of the Nuns had done work in the French Orders as Teresa Angelica and Celeste Marie.)

"My child, let us never again look back to That Day. But let us join hands to go forward, for the greatest battle is yet to begin. You will stand in that battle, and inspire others to stand beside you, but I will stand with you and when you speak I will be seen of them that know Me.

"When you raise your right hand to send the healing ray upon the people, turn back your palm as if to show a nail print in your palm. Beam your right hand across each seat as if to show a nail print in your palm. Beam your right hand across each seat in the auditoriums and they that are healed shall see the nailprint. For it will not be your hand but my Hand. It will not be your arm but my arm and they will know that it is I.

The Bottom Line

As I worked steadily upon this manuscript, the Great Central Sun moved into the Hierarchy Gemini in 1981. I sensed an undertow within me that something of importance was coming my way. Lord Jesus-Sananda began to come in very often and always seemed to be near. I meditated upon that old recall experience considerably, I felt there were still some answers to be given. For example I KNEW that I had been one of Apostle Phillip's daughters, at the same time with an equal certainty knowing myself to be that one at the Cross.

In early June Lord Sananda came, and talked with me for a very lengthy and informative conversation which I believe you will find interesting.

"Good evening, Tuella, I greet you in the Radiance of the One. I have come to bring you an explanation long overdue. You had heard your Father Phillip speak of these things and your sisters as well, but you My Love, held out for a making up of your own' mind. You gathered with the crowds and listened, but it was difficult for you to correlate it all into a pattern of facts understood and believed. But you continued to follow, always following, always listening, determined to understand. And then one sunny day, on the hillside, it happened to you. The Shekinah Glory struck you powerfully as you knelt upon your knees in brilliant Light and opened your arms upward to acknowledge your realization of Truth. Your rejoicing was a joy to all of us, to everyone and to the angels of heaven.

"You continued on with our company, and it was shortly after that I spoke in the house of Simon, that you ran in from the street to fall at my feet. You washed my feet with your tears of gratitude and wiped my feet with your hair. You poured precious and costly spices upon my feet and our followers, one in particular, grumbled concerning this. But I bade him not, for within My Being I knew that this was an anointing for My burial, and I bade you to continue, but the others knew not of the meaning. You had sensed this great gulf, this separation of dimensions, and in your sadness you had done these things that night.

"You followed with us continually and it was a natural thing that you followed along the side of the road with me, after the night of trials and anguish. You had kept your faithful vigil with the other women, outside the courts all of the night long. You listened in amazement as Peter denied Me and could not believe the others had fled. You remained close to My Mother and walked the path to Golgotha, by my side, at the edge of the road.

ON EARTH ASSIGNMENT: THE COSMIC AWAKENING OF
LIGHT WORKERS, WALK-INS AND ALL STAR-BORN REPRESENTATTIVES

"It was in your moment of great concern that you broke ranks and came to My side to wipe My face with the new veil you had begun to wear when you became one of us. You had never covered your head before. There were many times when you cleansed My face when in times of heat and exhaustion it was necessary. It was always the three Marys who ministered to My needs.

"Through much confusion and error, the world has given unto this one a name that is false, making her into another person, but she who wiped My face was the same one who had anointed My feet; who thus removed her veil to wipe from My brow the grime from the long night in Pilate's hall.'

"At the hour of her great rejoicing on the hillside when she was struck prone, you, the Being Tuella, were permitted to take control of the form of Mary Magdalene who was sick unto death. You then guided the rest of that incarnation as Mary Magdalene into a ranking Master Teacher.

"The gift to you for the gesture of the veil, was an imprint of my image upon your cloth, to remain with you for the rest of those days. The legend as it is told today does have this element of truth in it. But it was Mary Magdalene who performed this act of Love to My Person in My darkest hour.

"You followed the carrying of My form with the others, until it was placed securely in the tomb. You remained longer, to weep through your vigil until sunrise the following day. It was a special gift given to you that you would be the first to receive the account from the Angel, of the resurrection of the body of your Lord. That you, a woman of devout faith and love, would as well, be the first Evangelist to go into the town and report to the others who gathered in their gloom, that I LIVED! This was My gift to you Tuella, in That Day, in that time, that this gift of announcement was given to you. Forever after that morning you also prophesied along with all of the others, and did teach the people, although the Law forbade that a woman should bear witness, yet you did bring your witness to all who would gather and listen. You remained with My Mother, and cared for Her also, along with John, until our work of that time was finished.

"Now it is time, and now we do another work, but for the same cause, that mankind would be awakened to see that all are the Sons and Daughters of God, destined to Greatness and Purity though in the physical form. Now all of our group of those days, have once again returned by oath and vow, and you have known some of them and shall know more of them before the work is done.

"I close now this message of revelation to you, which we have waited so long to give you. Tuella is the name from higher worlds (Tu-El-La, meaning 'daughter of the Gods') these other names are planetary, they come and go, it is the thread of devotion to Truth that is of importance and not the identities. I Am Jesus of Nazareth, Sananda of the Higher Planes of levels of Pure Light. I call you My friend."

I poured over the scriptures that speak of these many happenings, shaken for many days by the depth of emotional recall. Lord Sananda came many times to give supportive encouragement as I slowly absorbed this new parcel of information and the continuing memory cells explosion. Ashtar also visited me to contribute his help:

"There has been much secrecy and confusion involved in this veil situation over the centuries. The handkerchief was indeed administered to Him by Mary as she stepped from the throng to wipe His brow. In your Being, which is SO VERY CLOSE to Sananda, inwardly you know these things are true. Your Being has stood by His side so many, many times and has wiped the sweat of dedication, toil and care from His brow again and again. As Mary, you wept for many hours at His grave before realizing He had risen. What joy given you, to make this announcement. For the kindness of the handkerchief, the gift was given, to tell others. The lovely peach colored cloth was close to you from then forward. These new revelations are intended for print in your new book. They will warm the hearts of all who read the works of Light and Love. I am Ashtar."

I am still struggling with my revelation because it is new, just as most of you do with your own. Apparently the pieces keep coming into us all along the line. I am somewhat stunned by the concept that healings forthcoming from my raised hand will make a nail print visible to the healed soul. Evidently, not only was His Image imprinted upon my cloth, but upon my body I would bear His marks forever.

Humanity Versus Mastery

In the preface I profoundly stated, you are not alone in the humanness of it all. As thrilling and uplifting as our various personal unveilings may be, we must not lose sight of the octave in which we live, the present and the now. Even the Queen of Heaven or the King of Arcturus or whomever now on earth, must still pay taxes, have a drivers license, carry various and assorted personal credentials and records, get cavities filled, wear glasses, break a bone now and then, pay rent, et al. It goes with the territory. Repeat those five gusty words to yourself when the pathway is unpaved. "It goes with the territory! "

In the last decade or two, I have personally long since ceased to ask Lords of Karma "why" about anything. There is a reason, a purpose, behind everything that is permitted to touch a Child of Light. I may not know what it is, but I know it's there. That makes me feel very special, to know that Divine Government would so manipulate circumstances to arrange a temporary setting for my growth, or to test my insight, or to check out my attitude rating, or to assist me to become better acquainted with myself as well as others. Again, perhaps my trial is for the benefit of another (John 1 1:1-14). Perhaps our suffering is permitted for the growth of another soul who is very special. Not even an accident can harm us except it be permitted.

We live in an octave in which humanity is a part. We must learn to accept our humanity and the entire perimeter of that implication. We volunteer to enter in full awareness of its limitations. Did not the writer of "Hebrews" (whom they say was a woman name Priscilla) write that the Great Master was "in all points tempted like as we are," referring to the acknowledged humanity of the Beloved Avatar? Did not the Apostle say, "We have this treasure in an earthen vessel?" PONDER THIS. For the Great Central Soul of you has occupied many a charnel house only to lay them all aside, but you my friend, go on forever.

We are the reflection of the octave in which we abide, AS 'WELL as the one from which we have COME! We are subject to this dimension BUT WITH A DIFFERENCE. Make no apologies for your humanity, rather, thank God for your Divinity. Because we have taken on humanity, we can accomplish what Angels cannot do! Without having become a part of humanity our mission would be pointless.

Therefore, expect those times when in spite of the goal of your Oversoul, in spite of your origin, you will be criticized; you will be silenced

ON EARTH ASSIGNMENT: THE COSMIC AWAKENING OF LIGHT WORKERS, WALK-INS AND ALL STAR-BORN REPRESENTATTIVES

by the brush of an ignorant hand or a careless hand. You will be "put down" by the cruel, disrespectful, discourteous word. You will be psychologically isolated, as it were, for your humanity, for many reasons.

Do realize that in those times, your humanity is but one spoke of the Wheel of your Being; a spoke that leads from the periphery of existence inward to the Hub of your Great Central Self, the TRUE YOU. Only at the periphery of the Wheel comes the rub of painful encounters and your human sufferings. The Highest evidence of your Divinity is to echo inwardly His words: "Father forgive them, for they know not what they do, they know not what they say," for the cruelest exposure is the loveless, unkind judgement of others.

* It is the hallmark of Mastery to be Christlike at those times when YOU DO NOT UNDERSTAND.

* It is a far greater hallmark of Mastery to be Christlike at those times WHEN YOU ARE MISUNDERSTOOD.

* We walk the pathways of the snare of the fowler but we walk with folded wings.

* Our physical temples house a GREAT GUEST.

Our earthen bodies are the platform of embodiment's expression. On our aircraft, our highways, our city streets, our fields of combat, we enter dangerous arena, but HE GIVETH HIS ANGELS CHARGE OVER US. We live in two worlds; one at a time. There are reasons which reason cannot understand. We walk in dignity aware of our divinity, conscious that, although in this world, we are not of it.

Lord Michael of the GREAT CENTRAL SUN, has dictated to me this message on the subject of Mastery which says it all:

"From our dimension come the 'Great Cosmic Teachers with their messages for the world, and many times in physical presence for a period of time. Their Presence is marked primarily with a quiet and long-suffering demeanor, a tendency to defer the last word and the winning statement, desiring, rather, to be docile and reflective, not given to verbal combativeness or self-acclaim. If they are wise (and they are), they will be the last to indicate this degree of awareness, so stand they unnoticed in the crowd and loathe to draw attention to themselves. There goes forth from them an emanation of penetrating quality that makes it comfortable to be within their aura of peace and stillness, while bringing conviction to those of much noise and much tooting of their own trumpet. For the silent ones, no such activity is necessary. They know who they are; they have nothing to prove, and seek not the limelight of praise for their understanding. It flows from them quietly, impregnating the atmosphere of their influence without the fanfare of words.

"They manipulate the circumstances which surround them by their silent mastery and undeniable contact with the twelfth plane of power. It is not power as the glory seekers use the term. It is the Power of Love and the power of indisputable Hierarchical corrections that direct the flow from the inner light that fills them. These are indeed the Lights of the World which hold all things in balance. Beware of the noisy ones, but listen closely to those who speak softly and speak seldom, for they will have something to say. Listen well to those who are themselves good listeners, for they have absorbed the wisdom. Those who proceed forth from the Hierarchy are themselves known of one another by a quiet blending of vibrations and a knowing that goes beyond all need for explanation of details. None are necessary.

"They will not engage in argumentative discussion of profound subjects, realizing that any convinced against his will is not convinced at all; his conviction must come from within.

"Truth bears witness of itself, recognizes itself and reflects a family resemblance in the manifestation of itself.

"This is the Mastery and the power that will defeat the most blustering adversary and overcome them by the quietness and confidence of the Inner Being. The Armour of God, or of His Light, is not only invisible, but is invincible, and these are the ones whose knowledge of this fact is built into the very warp of their Christ Selves.

"Their noncommittal stance often draws to them an offensive persecution, which does not disturb their peace. They will bless the voice that curses them and kiss the hand that delivers the blow, while bathing their opponents in Light.

**ON EARTH ASSIGNMENT: THE COSMIC AWAKENING OF
LIGHT WORKERS, WALK-INS AND ALL STAR-BORN REPRESENTATTIVES**

"They will listen respectfully to long tirades of argument and human wisdom, then quietly sum up a simple response in but a few well-chosen words of Truth, in simple parable or paradox. They avoid the crowds, though the crowds seek them out, but they will not accept any credit to themselves, reflecting only the Father who doeth the works. They will acknowledge the Christ in all, and the seeds of Truth in all divisions upon the pathway, knowing that all souls will at some point find their own truth of the moment, then pass on to greater truth.

"Mastery is the quiet control of the inner man and outer circumstances of life through the influence upon the inner planes. The man who has conquered himself can stand as conqueror in any situation, and quietly so. The awareness of the Master encompasses all of the unlimited access to his or her spiritual Oversoul, and hinders it not. Masters need to find awakening and pull their truth through their human consciousness just as any other soul must do, but their progress is swifter in this unfoldment. Whether suddenly or gradually is totally irrelevant in the final manifestation of the Christed Being walking the paths of this world. Become the Master that you already are ... where you are. None stand alone. Others are always near, in the shadows, and in the moment of Truth. Be vigilant against the rising tide of darkness. I am Michael, of the Great Central Sun, administrator of the Divine Program for this Universe. My blessings upon all who are realizing their source and their mastery at this time. "

Life's Highest Equipment

Divine Power

Chapter 4

The Cycles of Life

A great philosopher taught his students, "Know thyself." This is a knowledge well worth striving for. To know why we are behaving a certain way at a specified time, or why specific events are pressing us in some specified area. We experience our truth, our conception of reality, simultaneously on all levels, and react to it from all levels of consciousness.

We are influenced by events and cycles we have very little control over, if any at all. Lord Monka taught me these things. He stressed that often the most we can do is to be intuitive and receptive and to know how to react in a balanced manner. He taught that this stewing, boiling, smelting pot, of characteristics that come out during instances of greater pleasure, is the way of life.

"A week and passive mind will retreat in actions of insecurity in moments when pressure is being applied. But strength of character and commitment always rises above the situation ultimately, in acts of mutual love for the benefit of all concerned.

"It requires great courage to perceive and discern and to rise to those instances. We can never be truly certain of what is taking place when we are at our worst, no more than we can discern the pains and sorrows experienced when we are at our best. We must regulate and balance in our discernment of ourselves. Know your cycles. It will strengthen you."

ON EARTH ASSIGNMENT: THE COSMIC AWAKENING OF
LIGHT WORKERS, WALK-INS AND ALL STAR-BORN REPRESENTATTIVES

Discovering and applying the various cycles of life is a fascinating and rewarding adventure. I began my quest with the simplest of them all, "Biorhythm." By now it is not news. Most all of you know of it and have found it dependable. I am told by the astrologists it runs side by side with the astrological indications also. Upon questioning, the teachers spoke of it in this way:

"The rhythms of the body are not theory. They are fact. Even the living cell of life carries rhythm and the souls and spirit fluctuate. All of life is a moving force. Only the dead are stilled. Even then the pulsing energy returns to energy. The many uses for this information make the study of biorhythm, so called, beneficial." [I asked concerning the relationship of biorhythm to astrological influence?] "Are not those based on definite predictable patterns, inevitable and precise in their courses? Biorhythm is but a scientific charging, so to speak, of a course that is determinable from the moment of birth."

We are ever mindful of the fact that the fifth principle of Hermes states:

"THE UNIVERSE IS RHYTHM. Everything flows out and in, everything has its tides; all things rise and fall. The pendulum swing manifests in everything, rhythm compensates. This principle of neutralization applies in affairs of the universe, suns, worlds; in life, mind, energy, matter. There is always an action and reaction, an advance and retreat.

Based on the fact that "...we need all the help we can get," and before the computerized biorhythm charts we have today, I prepared by hand, graph charts regularly for every family member. We studied the effects and were amazed at its uncanny accuracy, even to the crabbiness of the siblings.

My husband had a troublesome heart condition at that time, but had a driving compulsion to build us a house. Working with his biorhythm chart, he only drove up to the property to work when his physical cycle was above the line, at its best. He rested on the crossing days, and stayed away from the project when the energy was low. With this reconciliation practiced faithfully, he completed our house, its wiring, plumbing and all details, and in a happy person for having done so. There was no threat to his physical welfare through it all. Personally I was most interested in the

ON EARTH ASSIGNMENT: THE COSMIC AWAKENING OF
LIGHT WORKERS, WALK-INS AND ALL STAR-BORN REPRESENTATTIVES

mental cycle, the green line cycle. I found that writing, channeling, and all creative work, flowed so effortlessly if I waited for those blessed 15 days of high mental energies. You can also have-a workable tolerance for your irritability if you are aware of those cycles of emotional upheaval that beset us all. It is easy to learn, since its 28 day length always has its biweekly "touchy" days. When you "know your cycles," you know when to do or not to do various things for the best results.

I had been an ardent fan of moon cycles for many years and always had one of the most beautiful gardens around because it was totally a moon sign occupation. (Of course talking to the elementals in the garden also contributed.)

Although I had never had the time to pursue astrology in depth, nevertheless I always applied all that I could master in a most serious way, and followed the planets in their courses across the sky religiously in their application to my own personal guidance. When my personal guidance system from other dimensions was set into place I no longer needed the astrology, but I am proud to say I have brought forth one astrologer in the family.

I recall the time when I was being taught the ebb and flow of the spiritual tide. I could not understand them, why at times the horizon of development seemed to recede farther and farther away like the tide of the ocean; withdrawing, only to return in a crescendo of power. I thought there was some lack in me, but it was all part of their training.

"You must learn to wait for us to open your seasons of fullness. We habitate the emptiness, though you know it is now. Watch your cycles and take note of them."

Then they shared with me which were my "best" months and which were the unfavorable ones. As I looked at them, a new revelation was given which I am delighted to share with you.

Take a blank sheet of paper and lay it crossways in front of you. Draw a straight line from left to right across the middle. At the extreme left of the line print your birth month and date. In the exact center of the line, print the month and date for exactly six months later. At the extreme right of the line print the month and the date of eleven months later.

ON EARTH ASSIGNMENT: THE COSMIC AWAKENING OF
LIGHT WORKERS, WALK-INS AND ALL STAR-BORN REPRESENTATTIVES

Now, in a manner similar to the daily biorhythm charts, add in the rise and fall line of your year cycle, giving the first six months as the upper cycle and the last six months as the lower cycle. Then we will add in the quarterly months so that all four quarters are charted.

For an individual born on, say, May 28, you will readily see that the high of the year for this individual is June through September, the best period for an extrovert type of push for all projects.

October and November will still be fairly well, but with a lessening of the power of the other months. Toward the end of November will be a critical time, a time for extreme caution in personal affairs, a time for withdrawal and recharging the batteries, so to speak. This is a planing time, a studying and evaluating time, preparatory for the big push of the coming June. The last six months of your year might not be favorable for planning a honeymoon or beginning a new business. You need to study your own life details to apply the knowledge.

In retrospect, consider past events of severe illnesses, heavy personal problems and rough going, and consider when they occurred. Review past great triumphs, promotions, career highlights or personal victories and take note when they occurred. I'd love to hear from you on how this year cycle works out for you. Apply the chart first from the physical standpoint. Then do another from the emotional standpoint and another from spiritual experiences. If a pattern emerges for you, you will then know more about yourself and your cycles.

The Runner and the Track

I learned of another yearly cycle in my sojourn with the Rosicrucian teachings. One of many cycles featured in a book called *Self Mastery with the Cycles of Life*, by H. Spencer Lewis, has information concerning the Cycle, which is most interesting and easy to apply. In this cycle, the year is divided into seven segments of 52 days, and these become the seven cycles of the personal year. Each segment of the seven has a totally different application. I recommend the book if you are interested in pursuing the use of cycle information.

Then of course, we have the greatest cycles of all, the courses of the personal planets as they weave in and out of the houses of our personal charts. The Teachers discussed this with me:

"The zodiacal patterns are laid before us as roads to travel in much the same way a handicap race is run by some runners. Just as the high jumper must continually compete against his own height, so the soul must continually face a new set of challenges to be perfected in the race that is before it.

"Each set of zodiacal patterns contains totally different situations for the soul to meet, as well as different influences with which to meet them. The soul goes through these patterns not once but as many times around the cycles as may be necessary. Higher affinities place one in higher influences of a particular cycle. For this cause you have the higher or positive influences and the lower or negative influences of a certain sign. This becomes the indicator of how many times around the cycle. We must run our race within a laid out field astrologically, just as the runner must run within a given place, for a given time and a given length. It is not so that some races are long and some are short? For some only a small time is needed for a certain cycle, thus the life is short lived, but necessary. The mystery of sudden or natural death to those of youth and great goodness or promise had held the meditation of philosophy for centuries. But there is the answer. Only the short time was required, for there is order in heaven.

"Every soul will face somewhere a given set of problematical circumstances. Some hesitate or fall by the wayside or develop delaying karma. Others are heroic of soul and proceed with victory where another would falter, and inherit to themselves karmic riches for future testings. It is a race that is set before us, determined, destined, measured, judged and rewarded.

The Cycle of the Soul

In 1984, 1 learned of yet another cycle:

"January of 1972 began a new cycle for you. [That was the year of my husband's fatal auto accident.] A totally different dimension of awareness was allowed to enter your experience. One full cycle of 12 years has now been completed. In the higher planes of Heaven World, a soul cycle is completed every twelve years that pass. This brings the month advent of

ON EARTH ASSIGNMENT: THE COSMIC AWAKENING OF LIGHT WORKERS, WALK-INS AND ALL STAR-BORN REPRESENTATTIVES

your new initiation, yet another dimension higher in responsibility, then anything that has gone before. You now hold the lamp of Light over an entire nation and the World."

I was told that for the Earth Volunteers (the "Nine's"), the soul cycle of 12 begins after the ninth birthday is completed. This is a soul cycle and not to be confused with the seven year incarnational cycle of Rosicrucianism which deals with circumstances of an earthly nature.

At that same full moon of January, 1984, there was an unusual variation as I was told that Seven Magicians of wisdom would speak with me. A very lengthy salutation in an unknown tongue was given.

It was more like a chanting prayer. All seven were in a kneeling position, not in my room, but in another ritualistic setting. I could see flame and smoke arising from their mouths as they looked upward and raised their hands. Soon they ceased and were silent, until One spoke:

"O daughter hear our words. It is given to thee to receive of the wisdom of the ancients and the magic of the knowledge of forces and causes, as they proceed forth from the central heart of God. Move within the inclinations that come to thee and fear not to venture into untrodden pathways. Yield thyself to the winds of change that will come to thee, to blow thee into deeper waters of experiences and knowing. We pronounce over thee the holy words of old; the initiation of fire and the tongue of fire is given you that your words shall flow as flame. So receive you the tongue of fire and word of power to be thy force for this cycle. Receive the crown of fire to circle thy head that the flame within thee perish not, for great is the need of thy words to this people.

"We the Circle of Seven Magicians of Wisdom, blow upon you the breath of Divine Fire, touching your spirit, your mind; your vision and determination to fulfill that which lies before. We send you these words in the Authority of the Great Central Throne, as one whom they have sent to accomplish the pouring out of their words in power. Receive thee this breath of fire into thy Being and let it burn within thee forever. We, the Circle of Seven, anoint thee for the cycle that is before you. It is done."

Then another lengthy chanting took place as I felt the weight of their hands upon my head. I remained quiet and still, awed by the moment and feeling that there was more to come. Then the vibration of dear El Morya came in with great power.

"We salute you daughter of the Light. All send you greetings and most high blessings in the sign of the heart, the head and the hand. I come to you in Spirit this way to honor your initiation as one who has volunteered to stand at the gates. We bring you the golden staff and the purpose robe of Authority on Earth. We bring you our following of loyal helpers who will serve with you to the end. I am El Morya. It is I who administer the Ray of Divine will and Power. It is I who will safely take you and yours through the events to come.

"The days before you are filled and busy and you are thrive on it as well as glow all the brighter. You have touched the secret of the ages and that is the understanding that you are our point of contact in all that we must do. We constantly look for outlets and dependable channels, but time is now short for preparing them. Realize that it takes a minimum of 12 years to prepare a voice who will consciously serve the Council. We have chosen you because you have chosen this embodiment instead of your further Ascension which you have earned. Therefore understand that the authority which is given is your own and not a delegated power. You may challenge evil wherever you meet it, and the Ascended Host and Angels will respond to your call. You may loosen the shackles of karma from your students and pierce them with your Light of Love, knowing you also hold the key to bind on earth and it will be done in heaven, but you will only use this power in the war against ignorance. Use it for bursting the chains of bondage and use it in the name of God, I AM THAT I AM."

Come Fly With Me

It is fun to sit around with other Earth Volunteers and swap stories of nocturnal excursions to other worlds. In the beginning the neophyte is considerably hung up on the idea of a physical excursion, a physical contact. An eyeball-to-eyeball conversation seems to be the most important thing in the world at that stage. Many years ago as Lucy Colson and I were discussing this on the telephone, Lord Joshua interrupted to chide us, using Lucy's mental power to do so:

"Why do you girls think you need this contact? You have just come from life upon the ships, you are with us every night, you speak with us continually. For you to insist that you need or want to speak physically with a Space Person is inconsistent and unnecessary!"

Apparently bizarre promises of physical experiences are given to maintain our early interests and to correspond to our level of understanding. For the deeply dedicated Eagles, here directly from the Commands, there is a better way. Let us recall the words of the Being Tuella who spoke under hypnosis with Dr. Sprinkle concerning "trips" to the Spacecraft:

"These experiences are necessary for my continuing contact, service, and understanding in this dimension. I do not feel comfortable here; I must constantly refurbish and strengthen my ties with my sources to continue here. My home is away from here and I must return often as is exemplified in the physical life here. There is a love and a longing for home. I am an alien in this land, but I must forbear, and I must continue my contacts with home."

We are aware that one of the severest trials for the young man sent off to war in our dimension, is the separation from those most dear to him and all of the environment he loves. His morale is held intact by those loving letters from home. Likewise our own out-of-body experiences are gifts of love to us to strengthen our ties to our sources. I love to have them talk about it.

"Your trips to our ships, especially your own Starship, are far too numerous to mention in detail. Nightly you return to us to carry on with us in this parallel life amongst the stars. You can identify these times in part by those nights when there is scarcely a stirring of your form during sleep; so much that a stiffness is produced and experienced upon waking. Nights when the form continually tosses and turns are usually indicative of human sleep and possibly very short-lived moments of excursion. On those nights of sound deep, long periods of sleep, you have been 'away' for an extended period of time.

"I can tell you of your body sometimes being lifted by invisible means while a counterpart has been left in its place. In this case the counterpart may turn and relax and even snore a bit to prove you are there. There are times, extended times, when you are with us. Your inner mind track has recorded such things but they are not released into the human consciousness because it is unnecessary at this time. Anything that needs to be released can be pulled through by quiet reverie and meditation on a given area. You are attired in your usual full flowing white garment, gathered with a golden girdle somewhat in the earth Grecian manner, and grasped at the shoulders with two circle ornaments embossed in special symbolism pertaining to your service on the soul level. In this capacity, you are Tuella of the Higher Worlds, very tall and the hair is full length of bronze tints on gold; not a yellow but a blend of golden browns and gold. The eyes are your own as they have always been. The eyes of an individual seldom change until the very uppermost degrees of dominion are inhabited permanently. Then eyes have many colors as beams of vital rays in action.

"The action of your eyes on the physical level also have very powerful rays impregnated into your physical orbs so much that your straight gaze into the eyes of another can pierce and read their soul. Sometimes they are aware of this but most times they are not. When you are in doubt or ever desire a deeper insight into a person, simply gaze steadily into their eyes, for this is a special gift you have. It could be compared to a spiritual x-ray of sorts, but you must be consciously using it for it to activate. This is not clairvoyance. It is a seeing into the soul reflecting back to you the character of that person or the discussion of the moment. You cannot be fooled when you do not desire to be. Your discernment of character and truthful speaking is a gift ever present if you choose to operate in this capacity.

Strangers Away From Home

Information concerning these nocturnal experiences comes at unexpected times. For example, at a certain time I had asked the question, "Why do I so often want to just burst into tears for seemingly no conscious reason?"

"This is an emotional debris from some recent excursion with us. It can bring much unhappiness into the conscious physical life though the cause is not consciously known. So much of the time you do not want to return and must be urged to do so. But on the higher levels where you work, you bring back much inspiration with you. You have not been taken over by a 'space person,' so called, or overshadowed by any possession of another, you are yourself an implantation upon earth, a sent one and an emissary of the Brotherhood and Sisterhood of Light.

"Your lifestyle is not normal, and your life's choices, small or great, are not normal to the average citizen of your land, or your age or your walk of life. You are stationed among them but are not one of them. You are very tried by the need to constantly adjust to human emotions and human situations in which you must learn to become a part of the environment of humanity. You are endowed with powers that cannot be used at this time, because of limitations of your implantation upon the earth. But you are free to exercise them when you are 'away' and in your normal soul environment."

I was told by the teachers that a tremendous residue remains in our thoughts from these higher visits, which filters through to consciousness as guidance, intuitive ideas, directions and inspirations. I have always known that my intuitive feelings are practically infallible, without the benefit of words or details. I finally came to realize the reason for this. I was told that in times of crisis, a conclave is always carried on with you in attendance to present your input.

"You have been taken in almost continual rendezvous for the last five years. There you have met and talked and been in conference with most of us who otherwise speak with you telepathically. Later telepathic rapport is enhanced by your meetings with us on these other occasions. There have been times when a copy of yourself has been left while you were away. You are consciously briefed on these substitutions so that nothing is unknown in your memory bank as might have occurred. You will be permitted to recall more of these things as time passes. Meditate upon these things and question your sources concerning this parallel pathway existence."

Parallel Pathways

Actually, I too often forget to ask about these things, but on occasion there are other pleasant means of confirmation. The Being, Obid, a friend and fellow Earth Volunteer who has been channeling for Ashtar's GOLDEN CIRCLE newsletter, once phoned me an account of a recalled out-of-body experience. Strangely enough, it arrived just in time for this chapter. He remembered being in the higher worlds in attendance at the Hall of Learning, listening in a most attentive manner to a lecture being given. He was electrified when he realized the speaker before the group in this faraway session was none other than his friend Lady Tuella. He had called as soon as he was awake enough to do so, and I also had some fragments of recall of having been there. These kinds of confirmations have been received many times and are always encouraging.

I have received many witnesses of bilocation when I have been in deep prayer, intercession or meditation for a person in need. Reports have filtered back of my having been clairvoyantly seen and recognized in the room with them. I suppose the intense emotional projection to the person and their location does this.

A very close friend and my "house" E.T. guardian, Captain Avalon, told me:

"There have been many times when you have been escorted as the body slept, as real as any physical journal. For example, you were permitted to totally recall your visit with Soltec when you viewed the Future Time track. You were permitted this recall, because of its usefulness to others."

This is an interesting passage because the Future Time track experience is all written up on the front page of the second issue (September 1984) of *Universal Network*. The article begins, "As I prepare for this issue in quiet meditation, I was taken out of my body on a flight. My hands rested lightly upon the arms of two spiritual escorts." And all along I thought it was happening right then... but actually it was all being filtered back through triggered recall. The article goes on to describe in detail the craft entry and the approaches, the rotunda where Soltec's desk was positioned, his warm greeting, and his tour, and finally the three massive screens upon which I was permitted to see the future of Mother Earth. It details the beautiful Earth after it is cleansed, the activity of the Great Craft as they clear the dimensional portals, the beauty of the new vegetation, and finally the descent of the colossal City Ship to begin life anew. It is a fascinating revelation of things to come. Everyone should read it.

But instead of experiencing it then as I thought it was, it was a playback of a nocturnal excursion. Avalon continued:

"Most of these occurrences, happen to you during the full moon period when the Great Starship Ashtar has returned to you. A fragment of information is permitted to come through to satisfy your sitting appointments, but the bulk of that which is intended is recorded on your inner consciousness, in person. You will find that the midnight hour is your appointed time for problems and communications in person. You are an implantation upon earth, yet throughout your childhood you spent much time 'away' from your body with a substitute left in its place. Now when you are 'away' no one is aware of it, including your conscious Being."

On another occasion, a speaker explained that when we sit with them in the morning as the first task of the day, as Guardians of our soulstar and our planet, the strong force with which they come to us is propelled by the energies that are left with us in our nighttime visits with them. They have further stated that our lives are so often involved in unsettling experiences which would cloud our minds and create unnecessary confusion for us, if knowledge of these visits were permitted. Therefore, these details have to be withheld from us in our best interests. In another report to me this was given:

"There are sometimes those occasions when persons who have desired to be taken into our midst have been lifted by mutual consent, but then have had to have the memory blocked for the sake of their own consciousness. You are one of those. The times you have visited with us in our dimension have been many and often, but to leave all of those experiences vivid in your consciousness would disrupt your earth life and its mission.

"Nevertheless the principal topic of discussion, or the purpose behind the encounter, does seep through in the guise of hunches, intuition, and a clear knowing of a certain direction or step to be taken. It is very clear to the consciousness and you could not be talked out of it. These moments are times when the residue of times with us invades human awareness as inner guidance."

Those whose dedication to their mission of service to this planet, having come from other areas of sacrifice, have no need to fear abductions or any such infractions of human free will. For those who stand with us in our mission of Light, have an impenetrable fortress of protection surrounding us that no outsider of any dimension may penetrate.

I once had an out-of-body initiation leave its effects on the physical form with some upsetting symptoms. When I asked to have an early morning illness explained, I was told:

"It was not an entirely physical experience. It was a reaction to your having been exposed to an initiation on higher levels during the night that just passed. Initiations require an adjustment to be made within the physical form. You were a bit upset when you realized you were seeing clairvoyantly as if a certain valve had opened. Etherically speaking this did take place. You were administered with the technologies of the higher craft, your Mother Ship, and you will be physically a bit off balance for three days. This event was scheduled for you at this full moon period.

"The food taken this morning was rejected by the physical which still held the high frequency. If you had not contained yourself you would have lost your entire meal. You must eat very lightly the next three days to remain comfortable. You mentioned the intensity of your sleep, so deep, so long. This is because the entire period of physical sleep was spent upon the Mother Ship of Ashtar."

Full recall of all these wonderful experiences is not a natural thing. Neither is it intended to be, for our own protection. If the human could totally remember all of these marvelous happenings of the spirit when it is free, the spirit would never want to return. But return one must if the mission is to carry forward. Thus the experiences are blocked from the conscious reasoning mind so that the conscious life may continue in its fulfillment, unbroken by desires to lay it aside.

An Eagle's Credentials

Beloved Oriel, Angel of the upper heavens, came by authority of Lord Michael to relay this message just before my husband's translation:

"I bring you the sign of the Solar Cross. Under this sign you may receive all who come. The Solar Cross is given as a circle first and centered with an equal armed cross. Accept this sign and fear it not for it is the symbol of the closing day's activity in which the' earth will be cleansed and all things made new."

(Note at this point in time, I had never heard of the earthbased organization called the *Solar Cross*, started by Richard Miller. It was yet seven years before I was exposed to their literature.)

"We came to you at this hour in the enlightenment that is upon you and decree that henceforth in the power of the Lord's Hosts on High, that all power shall be given unto you and nothing shall be withheld from you. The scepter of authority is in your hand and in all moments of action and the spoken word you may call for the assistance of the Heavenly Host.

"We have been watching over you for many years and leading you to the awakening of truths as they must be given forth. A plan is in motion for your activities and mission. From this moment forward, know that you are being propelled by the Highest Christ Forces available to man on earth. Know that angels walk with you and authority is given for any situation."

At that point in time, every message ever received and recorded in my notebook was signed in a sweeping symbol of the circle and the cross symbol. This went on for several years until finally the use of the typewriter, in recording, would simply close with the words, *"Sign of the Solar Cross."* How I LOVED THAT SYMBOL. It was the mark of authority to me. It was many years later that I learned that a blueprint diagram of the round Mother Ship, when viewed from the top looking downward is an exact replica of the Solar Cross. The small center circle representing the power center of the craft, the four pathways or highways at the four compass points representing transportation routes within the craft to various sections of different levels, and the outer circumference circle roadway representing the main access highway within the craft, lined with elevators and providing access to any area of the craft. What glorious organization and order exists in heaven. The blueprint of their ships being the symbol of these latter days when they would become the Angels of God's Harvest.

The Big Computer in the Sky

A pleasant surprise came through one day concerning soul records. (The Name of the Master is withheld):

"It is an honor to present to you Master ____ whom you have not met before nor spoken with before. He comes to you from the 12th plane of reality. I introduce to you now Master ____.

"Good morning, Tuella. I do not feel that we are strangers, for we share many things of heart and mind. I am a close friend of Lord Kuthumi and all the others you know so well. My work within the Hierarchy is that of Superintendent of Records or reincarnations and the embodiments of souls upon not only Earth but other worlds of the same solar system as well.

"I come to speak with you because you have also shared in this kind of work between incarnations and your missions of service. As you know, the records of incarnations are tremendous in scope. Nevertheless they are all neatly and efficiently kept accurately in the great computers of higher dimensions. Whether one seeks by one name only of any incarnation or by heavenly names from other worlds, all of the information is there, complete and in detail. The soul itself may forget its other lives, its other names, but it is recorded never to pass away in the records of heaven. I am responsible for the upkeep and the maintenance of these records, for the access of all others who might need to refer to them. It is a fascinating task.

"In the judgment of the Karmic Board and the Hierarchical Board, it has been determined that you now be given that right to access of these records at will. Of course when not incarnate, you always have this access, but the embodied state which lowered the veils, removed access to the records until a certain point of evolvement."

"There have been isolated moments when, in the sheer power of your mind, you did not have access, but now we are opening to you this access officially and consistently. We do now relay to you this privilege as it may be needed by you in your service to others.

"The method employed in your access to this great computer will be to call me directly by name, the Doorkeeper of the Hall of Records. Now that I have blended with your vibration in this transmission, our tie will never be broken for this incarnation. Beyond that you will no longer need it. You may use the soul's planetary name of this time to make your request and I or one of my many thousands of assistants will respond with your file.

"You need not state the reason for the request. Simply sit ready to record and it will be freely given through the quasar communications system. Questions may be injected as needed. These are not life readings. These are soul records."

ARE YOU IMPLYING THAT I WILL BE GETTING INTO A KIND OF READING WHICH I HAVE BEEN TOLD NOT TO DO?

"Not necessarily. This is simply the authority for access to the records. It is an honor that must be earned by any teacher in embodiment status."

MAY THIS INFORMATION BE PASSED ON TO THE PERSON?

"This may be done based on your own discretion and evaluation of the individual's ability to cope with it.

"You have in the past received much information from the records through others because they, themselves, had access which they shared with you. Now you have personal access without the help of another. That is the difference."

Life's highest equipment is in the endowment of spiritual power and all of its attributes. It is given to us to assure the success of the KINGDOM OF GOD on Earth, and our part in bringing it to pass.

We are Love in Action here ... and Love is the Power!

Close Encounters of the Tiny Kind

The gifts of God evidenced in the Earth-Based Volunteer are a joy to experience, whatever their manifestation may be. My daughter, Eve, is blessed with the ability to see and speak with nature spirits, the elementals of growing things. We have had many hours of pleasure in this kind of encounter.

My former home in Pennsylvania was surrounded in oak woods, a stream, and abundance of large ferns and many of them became good friends. The large oak tree, a triple oak coming up from one base, supported my swing, where I rested while the oak and I conversed. The great oak, it seems, was the supervising elemental of the property. I soon learned that if there was a problem with any growing thing, to come and ask "The Big One" what the problem was. I was concerned about strawberry plants which I had placed in a barrel with many round holes, one at each hole, and watering from the top. They didn't look happy and well. The Big One told me they were thirsty because the water lowered in the soil too quickly and left them dry. I remedied that situation by relocating them and received back a commendable report. The Big One also served as a guardian to me alone in the rural property.

ON EARTH ASSIGNMENT: THE COSMIC AWAKENING OF LIGHT WORKERS, WALK-INS AND ALL STAR-BORN REPRESENTATTIVES

One afternoon, Eve and I were roaming in a big park, just outside of the Capital area; and we decided to talk to the little fairies if any would come. They are so delicate, so small, and so lovely in appearance. So I gave the "call" and Eve was going to do the "seeing." She halted me, "Mother, you had better stop calling, you've rounded up an elemental convention. We're being mobbed."

In that area there was an abundance of a certain weed which had a twelve inch spread leaf. They were everywhere. Eve excitedly saw that three to four beautiful little fairies were on these large leaves, brilliant in their mixed colors and pretty adornment. She spoke with them, and they were honored to have been called and very happy to meet with someone who knew they existed. This particular group had large iridescent colored wings of a sort, that seemed to be color coordinated with whatever their garment was. They were about two inches high. There were other elementals there, out of the woods, who were larger, up to six inches, and dressed in a forest green. It was a wonderful convention that sunny day in the park.

There was one time in my Pennsylvania living room, when my vision cleared long enough for me to see scattered and sprawling, literally all over my carpet, little elementals that had come in from outside and they were either sitting cross-legged looking up at me, or leaning against a chair leg, or standing at attention, all staring at me. So I welcomed them and apologized for not having realized before that they were there. They smiled and said they liked my house, they thanked me for the vegetable garden which they helped with very much. They told me the moles had eaten my tulip bulbs and they were unable to prevent that. Some tried to climb up on my lap or chair arm, but I disciplined them to remain down on the floor. They understood and just smiled. Most of them had very round faces and large eyes. After that there were times when I worked at my chores outside and I sensed a column of them following me around. In my morning decree session, I had always included a decree for the elementals of creation. I realized after seeing them that they knew I loved them. The time came when I had to leave the property, and drive to Colorado Springs to join my daughter Eve there. I had a small station wagon and was able to crowd into it all of my houseplants, my cat "Little friend," and a large bucket filled with the biggest Boston Fern I could find along the creek which ran through the grounds. The property of much shade from the oaks, the mists of the mountains and the 'Moisture of the little stream was ideal for the mass foliage of ferns that covered the place.

After settling into our house in Colorado, one day following a particularly exhausting shopping trip, we kicked off our shoes and threw ourselves onto the bed to relax. Eve was looking upward to the bookcase headboard above her head and detected a lot of motion. She discovered that her favorite little houseplant had an elemental on it of exuberant energy. She struck up an acquaintance and we named him "Charlie." He was very young and he especially enjoyed having Eve's four year old "Deirdre" bouncing and hollering around the room and the house. We decided to get acquainted with all the others, going from plant to plant and talking to them, psyching out their appearance and what-not.

We spoke with one plant that had literally been in my life for a decade. A philodendron from which I had taken dozens of starts for new plants, but this was the original stalk.

It had traveled all over the country with my husband and I on his various projects. The little elemental, called "The Old One," was two inches tall, all bent and very aged. He asked if he could be moved upstairs to my bedroom because the noise and movement of Deirdre "drove him up the wall," so to speak. He wanted to be alone in a quiet place. We asked each plant if there was anything they wanted and so on. The bouncing boy admitted he wanted a puppy. Well that was a challenge, him being only a little over an inch high. We decided to check all the gift shops to find a tiny china puppy. It inspired us to ask them all what they would want. The little old man wanted a comfortable chair, a rocker, maybe, like mine. An adult couple with a larger plant who looked a bit rural asked to have a pair of horses. We joyfully made out our list and had great fun the following day bringing home their gifts. We found a china family of dogs out of which we took Charlie's puppy. So often after that Eve would see him resting against the puppy, or sitting on him or whatever. Anytime she checked the old one he was always sitting in his lovely tiny, overstuffed, blue china chair with a height of about two and a half inches. We were able to find the team of horses for the farm couple, and so it went, all over the house. It took several trips to find all of the things they had asked for, but they were certainly one happy group of little elementals. From time to time we would find little items to bring home to them. They loved tiny birds, and flowers, another one wanted a watering can. We finally did find one.

ON EARTH ASSIGNMENT: THE COSMIC AWAKENING OF
LIGHT WORKERS, WALK-INS AND ALL STAR-BORN REPRESENTATTIVES

But amidst all this joy there was a sadness as well'. Charlie told us that the big fern, called "The Weathered One" (an elder of female gender), was sick and in need of attention. She it was who appointed each one, including Charlie, and they all held her in awe and great respect. She was called only by that name, "*The Weathered One*," having sustained the fern through many, many a cold winter and changing season, even to a leadership of all the other ferns there, for she was the grandest of them all. We had her placed at first in a corner where we all constantly went by. She was weakened by being constantly showered by our auras as we whisked by. She had first asked for relocation. She was in such a weakened condition we placed her centered on the dining room table for protection space, along with two growths of Ivy cuttings from the old property. We learned that she was dying of heartbreak. We did not understand. We were told that she was their supervising elemental, being the largest of the crowd; that she was overcome with melancholia from having been torn up and transplanted into this hot, dry place. She longed for her environment in the woods; the chipmunks, the rabbits and birds, the mists of the morning and the shade of the oaks.

When Deirdre learned the plant missed the animals, she brought all of her miniature animals and lovingly placed them around the fern. The Weathered One was herself about three inches high; taller than the rest. Charlie instructed us to place all of the plants close around her to give her supportive consolation and energies, and it might help. This we did immediately and placed pans of water around her as well. It took about three weeks of this intensive care and loving ministrations, until she finally began to respond. When her strength permitted, we planted her on the shady side of the house outdoors around other growing things and she recuperated wholly. It was all a very educational experience.

A little elemental cannot get too distant from its assigned plant for very long, just a few minutes. During Charlie's stationing for the intensive care, he didn't like it when Eve and Deirdre watched TV upstairs, because he couldn't come up. He enjoys and watches TV. So Deirdre would carry him up for the occasion. One night they were watching Emergency, absorbed and certainly not thinking of Charlie. Within the story there was pictured a devastating fire and suddenly Eve realized that Charlie was jumping up and down on her shoulder, absolutely terrified! He had never seen fire before. The program ended and Eve had to talk with him at great length and explain a lot of things, specifically that he was not in any danger from

ON EARTH ASSIGNMENT: THE COSMIC AWAKENING OF
LIGHT WORKERS, WALK-INS AND ALL STAR-BORN REPRESENTATTIVES

fire, and so on.

These tiny elementals are living Beings who are each responsible for the growing things assigned to them; they are its life from the Cosmos. If we mistreat a plant, by not caring for it, watering it, the elemental will depart and the plant is left to die. When we talk of our plants, we are actually talking to the elemental who is its life, and your words are consciously heard and understood, particularly the love vibration they carry.

My favorite elemental story is about "Airella." I was at that time heavily into decreeing and the use of a household altar. I found a small plant for it, which in my mind would stand representative of the nature Kingdom on the altar. I found a small plant for it, which in my mind would stand representative of the nature Kingdom on the altar. I chose a modest size white sculptured pot. We carried it upstairs, placed it on the altar and sat quietly to watch. The elemental's name assigned to the plant was Airella. Details of any raiment were not discernible, only a brightness. Eve said she was "Dressed in Light." She descended gently down from the plant pot and floated around all over the altar, examined the big brass candle holder. She stood before the electrically lit figurine of the Divine Mother, paused in reverence before the Golden Angel, which symbolically represented the Angelic Forces. Similarly she stood in reverent pause before small figurines of Jesus the Christ and Guatama Buddha.

She was awestruck and overwhelmed by the honor of having been chosen as the elemental of the Forces of Light in the home. She was scheduled for ascension to a fire spirit, therefore had earned this responsibility as keeper of the flame on my little altar. We had just recently moved in, and the devotional spot was new. I was told to begin with very brief decrees and meditation periods, increasing them very gradually, so that the power of the focus would be released slowly until Airella became capable of carrying on the daily ritual. This was her training as well as her privilege. At Christmas I found a tiny Angel to join her with the plant.

I apologize for having digressed rather markedly from the remainder of the chapter material, but it seems to me that the power to bring back a unity of life with all of God's Kingdoms is a great step forward toward life as it shall be in the New Age environment. It is a manifestation of Love, and Love is Power.

Life's Highest Lessons

Divine Education

Chapter 5

Planetary Lessons

In the coming schedule of planetary lessons, it is a bit difficult even for the Celestials to pinpoint the sequence because of an overlap in the many changes before humankind. The Purpose in all end time events is Spiritual Education and growth of God Consciousness.

As these words are written, one of the major lessons upon the immediate horizon for humanity is the Lesson of Abundance. There follows a joint release from the Spiritual Hierarchy of the Ashtar Command. This represents a seven-day intensive communication endeavor directly from and in the power of the Throne Energies of Celestia, specifically ordained for inclusion in this book.

The committee of Speakers was composed of LORD MICHAEL., LORD JESUS SANANDA, LORD KUTHUMI, MOTHER MARY and COMMAND ASHTAR. The material was recorded and prepared for publication jointly by Hierarchical messengers Tuella and Obid, the first week of the ninth month of 1988.

Hierarchical Control of World Economy

We desire to stress the importance of economic pressure because of the impact it will have on the entire planetary specie. All humans are linked, in some way, to the world economic situation. The planetary specie is not capable of advancing itself without the reordering of the economic philosophy. Total surrender to the Higher Power must be the goal of the new economic policy for this planet before its final transition. The importance of this cannot be overstated. It will be seen in the coming months the necessity of addressing the economy in ways which heretofore have not been.

The economy is collapsing and winter schedule will follow. The economy has weathered what it thought was its biggest storm last October [1987] when the crash took place. This was a time of intense interest for those associated with market affairs. They were well aware that it could happen again.

It would have been worse had it not been for some very evasive action taken by those in the Spiritual Hierarchy who watch over these matters. They were certain there would not be time to react if the market continued to fall. We are pleased these matters stabilized long enough for these teachings to be brought forth. Otherwise the Economic Plan would have been aborted and you would have moved farther down the sequence of events. As it is now we can still bring forth the Economic Plan without sacrificing other parts of the planned schedule. This will not effect any part of the ultimate efforts for transition of the planet into hits next orbital frequency. The economy is being propped up with orders from the Most High, the Father Mother God. This intervention will not be repeated until it is absolutely necessary. That is not expected to happen with the economy, but could happen in regards to the Evacuation or other aspects of the Plan. You are being told this to assure you that the Father is not going to let anything happen to His Children that would prevent them from finding their Divinity which is the purpose of this whole exercise on the economy. Humanity must learn to turn all financial affairs to the father. This absolutely has to be introduced into mass consciousness.

The Domino Effect

The stock market has begun its permanent descent. You will see very little fluctuation as it continues downward until all is lost. The time is upon the planet. Winter will evidence that the markets are a sign of total collapse; a sign of days of much difficulty ahead. This market fall of colossal proportions will consistently plunge, but at a gradual pace and as a string of events. This will be precipitated by the action of the Federal Reserve, who are but pawns of the World Manipulators. But realize that even the action of the fallen ones must be permitted and allowed of the Heavenly Father. All things proceed forth from Divine Government for the necessary spiritual lessons. It is time for the secret manipulator Leaders to learn they can no longer be permitted to crush mankind for their own greed. Now the positions shall be reversed and the great cartels shall tumble. The steady consistent decrease will touch its dangerous mark in the holiday months, and a slowly arising fear developing within the Lords of finance. On about the tenth day of continual dipping, an identical process will begin in the great foreign markets. Thus gradually the entire system will become engulfed in the undertow. We reach the Manipulators with no escape for them provided. There will be ample time for souls to take heed and to take necessary steps not to be overcome by oncoming events. It must be remembered and continually understood that these events regarding the monies of the world citizenry is not intended to be disaster, although it may appear to be so. The intended chastening is geared to selfish interests that abound.

Vast kingdoms of economic control will find themselves in a boxed-in situation from which they cannot extricate themselves. This will be reflected in local industrial situations as it spreads from one industry to another, but those who have heard our words and trusted our guidance will be secure from the upheaval. Those who are touched by it will be those most in need of the lesson involved.

The Investment Market

The economic policy that must come into place will be the result of complete chaos in the financial markets. The IRS and the Federal Reserve System will attempt to collaborate to prevent the disasters from happening, but they are already too late. That which they are presently instigating in the form of higher interest rates will be the final factor. The Federal Reserve cannot accommodate that which is about to happen. The Federal Reserve is a fallen thought form that must erase itself. We cannot nor would we interfere with this process. We do not change that which is wrong, as you might think. By infusing the Light into that which is not in Universal Harmony, it must correct itself.

The economy is already stretched to its limits in terms of productivity. When the higher interest rates appear to be on the horizon, there will no longer be an expectancy of expansion. This will then stimulate foreign investment in those industries which are no longer capable of expansion. This will in turn tie the world economy together so tightly that no industrial nation will be able to escape the downfall of American economy, resulting in global reaction.

One must understand how the worldwide economies will take to this change in the immediate future. The Japanese investment in this country, as well as other countries, is already well underway. It will be greatly amplified in coming months as more Japanese yen find their way into the American economy to ward off further drops in the dollar. Without a halt in the fall of the dollar, there will not be enough strength in the American system to prevent even the smallest economic problems. The value of the dollar has been rising and falling due to the government intervention and the buying and selling of dollars by the international banks. As long as this continues there will be a false sense of security in relation to the overall economy. Once the dollar fluctuates beyond the range where government and multinational banks can regulate it, then there is going to be permanent chaos.

This is the lever that is being used to temporarily pop up the international money markets, for without it the dollar would certainly collapse and this in the immediate future. Once it is determined that the dollar value is artificially kept high, there will be a rapid migration away from investing in it. This as a result of an awareness that the dollar is no longer supported by the government. Even your government must finally recognize its own insolvency. This will occur as growing demands for bailing out the farmers and others hit by the drought, and those in food production. Although inflation is being caused by the drought, the Federal Reserve is tightening interest rates, implying a heated economy or attainment of top production levels. Since this is simply not the case, this action alone will be enough to topple the whole economy.

When God Removes His Hand

The people will soon see that the fallen ones who have been controlling all of the planetary economic activity will no longer be able to support it without the God-Given Forces of Light. This will be evident when the final collapse comes and the old solutions are no longer viable. No longer will the government be able to borrow its way out of the problem because the banks will no longer be able to lend money. Money will not be available to the banks and the printing of more will not be possible because the banks would not have the ability to move useless money back into the economy.

This is partly due to the lack of confidence on the consumer side of things, but also the result of international markets that have been the only ones which have actually been keeping things afloat. The international banks will not be able to continue this for very long because they will deplete their own currencies which further contributes to international economic downfall.

So first we have the failure of the American economy; then the failure of those of other major capitalistic countries; then those of the rest of the industrialized nations follow; finally, those of the underdeveloped nations. Surprisingly, these will be the least effected by the chaos. They have already learned the economic pitfalls of capitalism and the borrowing system. They will be able to make do with less a lot easier than the industrialized nations who have been abusive of the abundance the Father has given to enjoy. One can see the potential for economic ruin in the lives of those who have grown accustomed to wanting to have more. They will have much difficulty until they turn their lives and financial concerns over to God.

The Fallen Ones Revealed

Things must be improved on the planet with the economic vehicle. This vehicle is the source of all the problems man currently has. He has been led to believe the "more" comes through the economic process. This is not the case. The only reason there is anything is because of the Father Mother God. Man has absorbed contaminated thought forms of the fallen ones and bought this economic theory which leads humanity farther away into spirituality. Now that we introduce this to the masses through some very creative economic conditioning, we further use it to allow the fallen ones to reveal themselves. They will be hard pressed to fight off the coming economic crisis without revealing to the masses that they have in fact perpetrated this economic situation for their own benefit. They have been masterminding the complete economic control of the planet for such a long time, that they have lost sight of the fact that man would someday be faced with a choice. That choice would be either the path of Light or that of darkness. As darkness falls over the economic environment, it reveals itself in such a way that man will have a clear choice. We see this as not being too difficult from our perspective. The fallen ones are now making their last stand in the physical plane. They will move to strongly control planetary situations

ON EARTH ASSIGNMENT: THE COSMIC AWAKENING OF
LIGHT WORKERS, WALK-INS AND ALL STAR-BORN REPRESENTATTIVES

through the approaching economic disaster.

(Note: It was on the third night of the ninth month of 1988 that the total cleansing of all the upper worlds of fallen ones and their presence and influence there on all other dimensions, was totally and finally completed. The upper and lower astral and all points beyond are no longer their permitted territory. All are now present upon the earth for their final days which they know to be short and fatal to their goals.)

In the Divine reversal of their plans, these earthbased fallen ones will represent the most formidable obstacle. Their influences and control includes the ENTIRE monetary system on this planet. There is no institution regarding money, that is not controlled by the fallen ones. They will not give up easily, nor will they allow the truth to be unfolded without a battle. They represent those who are against the Light. They take bodies from all nationalities and it should not be considered that any one nationality represents the dark ones, for that is an untruth. This has been another of those misteachings by those unawakened brothers preaching the gospel of misinterpretation.

The fallen ones in this physical dimension can only play by the same rules that earthlings have to adhere to. While they were in the higher realms they had power over you in that they could manipulate the Divine thought forms. This caused many Light workers to receive confused data from above. Now that they are in your realm you can extinguish their energy by just remaining in the Light. They cannot handle your Light. They cannot tolerate the vibration of your soul, nor can they handle the Love you project. Our work now shall be much easier since we no longer have the influences of the fallen ones to deal with in the higher realms. This is important because in the past we were opposed by the fallen ones and were not permitted to interfere with those who were in control of this planetary region.

Channeling will still be only as clear as the channel permits it to be. Most channels have not yet freed themselves up from their own misguided thought forms and mental or emotional hang ups. This interior and inferior baggage will still bring in interception and interference and subterfuge to the unprepared channel. It is decidedly important now that one does not attempt to channel for others until all of one's Being is open and flowing in abundance of clearance and purity, because of this intensive last stand of the fallen ones on earth, and their determination to seed confusion in the minds of mankind.

The New Plan

The Plan calls for the implementation of a completely new method of doing business. The existing format will no longer succeed. The Plan calls for a new currency exchange that will be solely controlled by the government and not by any financial centerpiece grouping. By this we mean that in the past the Federal Reserve and other financial bodies have taken control of financial matters at the detriment of the government's ability to lead the economic policy.

With the Federal Reserve, the IRS and other government agencies no longer active, there is room to return sound economic policy to the system. This calls for free cash flow with eliminating debt burdens and without the need to address the past. This will be a very difficult concept for many to grasp. The free cash flow will result as the need arises to have an intermediary form of exchange. This crafts for a sound economic policy which will ultimately lead to the absence of money altogether. Then will be the freedom to move the soul forward in the path of Light evolution.

The concept of free cash flow is the only remedy to fighting back the dark forces who have controlled the economic policies for so long. Those of the Light will be familiar with the times that are upon us. We present here only a temporary solution, for the final solution comes with Love and final sharing of all of God's Abundance. The Heavenly Father is awaiting the call for bringing forth all of the Abundance necessary for all. It only requires the will of the people to make this call, for it to manifest. The times are now upon us to implement this new economic policy. That is why we have focused all of our Throne Energies and that of our messengers here involved, to focus on this problem and its coming solution. Once the government realizes that it can print money without the need to going through the financial markets then there will be a means to counteracting the works of the fallen ones. People will be receptive to the idea. What prevents man from realizing that the money is worthless in itself, is that it will be the only thing available to use as a medium of exchange. This will only need to be used for a brief period of time. As soon as mankind realizes that money doesn't need to be, then there will be a free flow of goods for the remainder of the time that they are on the planet. Realize that we are only discussing an extended period of time in your earth years. In only a blink of an eye, we will move into the higher dimensions in a moment, that is, those who have made plans to go. Government will not need to plan for the future in the third dimension, for the third dimension is passing and the fifth is entering.

We do not want to see this economic crisis happen before the New Plan is ready for implementation. It must be realized that without a Divine Plan, there would be no hope whatsoever in resolving the pending crisis. We do not suggest that there is no room for flexibility, but such can only come when all is made ready. Otherwise there would be no alternative but to let the system crumble and chips fall where they may. This has happened before, and it could certainly happen again. This is not a matter to be laid aside for a rainy day. It is upon you and must be dealt with until all is in order according to the Divine Plan. Just as the Planet must be balanced, the economic situation also must reach a point of balance before we will be free to inject Light into other areas of CHANGES and Divine Education. The Plan calls for COMPLETE ALLIANCE WITH THE SPIRITUAL HIERARCHY. We will be able to manifest whatever is needed in the physical plane once there is a call from those of you who are spiritually encoded with the willingness and responsibility to support the Plan. Many will remain lost in their own lower self consciousness. Much discernment will be required for the Light workers of this dimension.

The Purpose-God Consciousness

The purpose of this economic rescue, as we consider it, is to bring forth a greater consciousness of the Father! An awareness of the Father's willingness to support His Children in all ways. This will occur as long as His children are willing to accept His help. This tremendous lesson has of course been implemented on an individual basis through the corridors-of human endeavor, as generation after generation has been subjected to their small personal economic educational crises. And on that individual basis the education of humanity has crawled along its path of progress. But now it is the time we must reach for the masses in this ongoing Lesson.

World economy has technically been in default for quite some time. The Plan called for it to go under some time ago. Without the artificial props of the Spiritual Government of humanity, there would have been no hope for it to remain solvent this long. This information is released to permit humanity to become more aware of our efforts on their behalf. We have

ON EARTH ASSIGNMENT: THE COSMIC AWAKENING OF
LIGHT WORKERS, WALK-INS AND ALL STAR-BORN REPRESENTATTIVES

done everything to forestall this event, so that the Father could use the economy as a starting point of the final transformation process. This has always been the Plan but it was not fully known whether or not the Plan could be implemented in such a way to bring about positive aspects for the awakening process in mass consciousness. It has always been known in Biblical prophecy that the economy would collapse. What was omitted was the possibility of its use for further awakening the people.

The present need is an open forum and discussion with the people concerning the lesson to be learned involving money. Those who have already absorbed this lesson will be untouched by the learning aspect of the financial disaster. What is to come before the close of this century will pale the events of 1929 in its magnitude of consequences. For this event will usher in sweeping changes and circumstances which will turn the hearts back to the Father for trusting His Love to provide their needs. A spiritual revival of tremendous magnitude will engulf the hearts of humanity to prepare them for further lessons in growth yet to come. For that time which remains to prepare for a new dimensional life is growing shorter every moment and graduation is in sight. Let the students prepare themselves.

This lesson for mankind must be assimilated into the Higher consciousness that the answer to want and need is not money. Mankind must be healed of its attitude to money and position it is given in human life here on earth. There are many covenants and promises which cover these needs within the Holy scriptures and writings of all the great world religions. One must instead look to that need which money would seemingly provide, by reversing the attention from money to its goal, then men can walk with God in total trust than those needs shall be given and that every want shall be supplied. This is the lesson that man must absorb, individually and collectively, before the planetary ascension into life beyond this passing age. For the world economic nightmare of this day shall not be found to have any place in the Golden Age to come.

In those parts of the earth where famine and disease start to manifest, there will be a certain consciousness surfacing in those areas that has not been prevalent on the planet for a long period. This will be particularly interesting to witness for those who have not seen true devotion to the Father Mother God. This has been seen in the Midwest drought area where prayers and faith are beginning to take over. This is nothing to compare with the spiritual renewal to take place in those locations which reflect total devastation. It is unfortunate that the planetary specie will not be able to ally behind those God forces to awaken to the Father's Presence.

As long as Earthbased Volunteers and Light workers remain in the Light these events to come will not touch them. It is only when one is coming through the awakening process that the fallen ones can influence the process. We do not allow any of God's Children to be affected by the dark forces unless of course it is of their own making. These are the thoughts of fear (of anything) and doubt that enters the minds of earth peoples. There is always the possibility of creating one's own darkness, if faith does not hold steadfast.

The most important step to take in reaction to individual, collective, national or international financial crisis is to pose the question, "What is the LESSON?" The driving force of any discussion of this chapter one may have with others, or a group, or an individual, or in your own thought world in the stillness of a sleepless night, or when your own budget is "going down the tubes" must be, *"What IS the lesson??????"*

Lessons from Mother Earth

We continue now with our comments on the coming events and the scheduling of them. It is a heart-rendering thing for us to look upon the scurrying of humanity with its abundance of mundane occupations as if this way of life were to continue forever. All who serve truth know this is not so, for this civilization is ending at this very moment. This world is on a collision course with drastic changes on every level of life. A listening world would immediately think storage of food, clothing, money and hard metal objects and so on. This would mean survival to them. But the only true survival is the spiritual welfare of the soul and its relationship with the Heavenly Father, for He will watch over and care for all His Children in any situation or emergency. Through the interference of the fallen ones before the final cleansing was recently completed of upper worlds, much of a wave of "new" information entering the planetary world has been totally distorted. The masses have been led to believe by some very popular sources that the planet will not undergo the extreme change that is ahead. They have been led to believe that what is happening is just a wave of the future and all will be the same except for the changes in people's personalities (i.e., the war, hate, greed, as ideas that shall pass away). Of course it will be necessary to make the personality changes, but that is not enough.

ON EARTH ASSIGNMENT: THE COSMIC AWAKENING OF
LIGHT WORKERS, WALK-INS AND ALL STAR-BORN REPRESENTATTIVES

The change must come in the vibration of the planet and its specie. This will require a total change in consciousness that only those who are taking on their Christ bodies will be able to explain. This total change will be all-encompassing. No longer will there be any memory of those things of the past, for this shall pass away before the higher dimensions can be reached. We have tried to explain this in terms of reorganizing mind, body, and soul, into a new Being, but this is too foreign to most. They cannot understand how they can completely change and still have their identity.

This earth has moved severely in the far east regions and will begin to move dramatically in the west. This is the signal to move off the coast. The Light workers can hold back these change for only so long and then the earth must release the pressures that have been binding her. You will see many more signs of the earth moving in your coming years. The earth movements that came to Utah in August of 1988 were extraordinary in the sense that the earth is not very fluid in that area. This means that the earth shifts there will push greatly on the outer reaches of continental plates. You will begin to see direct correlations between each earth movement and what is to follow in another area of the planet. Action reverberates to the spot directly opposite on the globe ... two actions so to speak, due to the ley lines and the magnetism within earth itself.

Earthquakes will continue on schedule with the big quake in California due to hit in the very near future. This will be a time of much concern for many because the quakes that will begin to surface in the latter days and those which follow will gradually increase in magnitude, causing many to reassess their housing arrangements. All of these occurrences are warnings before the final one. We have made arrangements for those who choose to go through the death experience. We pray that many will choose to remain in their bodies so they can continue to use them in other areas of the universe. There is a great need for bodies in the physical dimensions and this is one reason for the evacuation. It will be necessary to evacuate all of those who wish to preserve their physical forms and not experience death again. This will greatly help in the soul development as well. Those who have listened and relocated to avoid further destruction represent a spiritual growth taking place. This is why Mother Earth has agreed not to release all of her pain in one giant event, although this does not mean that she will not have to do this in the near future.

ON EARTH ASSIGNMENT: THE COSMIC AWAKENING OF LIGHT WORKERS, WALK-INS AND ALL STAR-BORN REPRESENTATTIVES

Earthquakes have rippling effects throughout the planet which cause structures to weaken. This in turn causes dams to break, mountains to move upwards and valleys to sink. Realize that the planet is an orbiting body of Light which, though a series of actions has been darkened by the shadows of evil forces which have caused the planet's Light to become obscured. This darkening effect ha§ prevented the natural growth of the planet just as would happen to a plant sheltered from Light. If the planet is going to survive, it requires a great release of these negative energies to become free of its restrictions, requiring a stretching of sorts to loosen up density around it. It can then circulate its Light within and receive from external sources to enhance its growth.

The big earthquakes must happen, because due to the fallen one's influence, earth has been out of balance for considerable time, and must right herself on her axis, before she can transcend into the next dimension. The fallen ones have caused a limitation of Light to this region of space. Pressure built because of this is released by earthquakes. Earth needs much Light for sustenance and now with much Light pouring forth she is able to use it to correct all fault that has caused her great pain. These faults are literal ones in that they are the stretch marks from the birth of malalignment. This could have been overcome in other ways had it not been so long before the fallen ones were brought under control in the higher realms. Now it is time for correction and it must be expedient, to prepare for all of the high frequency changes upon the planet.

Other cataclysms will be due to man's karmic nature. The negativity he has built up over eons must NOW be balanced to bring all things into harmony before the transition. This karma can be overcome by his willingness to listen and respond to higher forces. Until recently there was no desire to do this. Now the presence of Abundant Light is going to change many. Much hardship comes because the work of changing men's hearts is overwhelming. Some areas are still in such darkness that this darkness can only be broken up by disasters. This is occurring in those parts of the world where flood and famine are reaching out. This will continue until the Light can touch the hearts of mankind.

Earthquakes will start in the Pacific rim and then be felt strongly throughout the planet. This has occurred recently in the wake of the Tokyo quake and subsequent effects in the Himalayas. This is but one round of many to follow.

ON EARTH ASSIGNMENT: THE COSMIC AWAKENING OF LIGHT WORKERS, WALK-INS AND ALL STAR-BORN REPRESENTATTIVES

The Greenhouse Effect

This is a good time to focus your love on the planet. She has been a good provider and now is the time for all of us to show our gratitude by allowing her time to reflect on the changes that are necessary to bring her into harmony with the universe. The first physical changes must be in the solar rays. All this discussion on the greenhouse effect has lost sight of the true reason for this problem. There is a need for the planet to warm in order to melt the ice caps and release some of the torque that has built up by these areas of water accumulation.

These polar regions have been untold stress on the planet and must be melted in order to bring about some greater balance. This melting will bring about a great release of water that will inundate the coastal regions. This has been prophesied by many and will come to pass in due time. The heating effect is what we must appreciate at this time. The increased temperatures will not be unbearable. Weather patterns will change but not to the extent that the whole planet will change overnight. It will effect how man feels about his environment which is a healthy transition.

Thoughts on the Evacuation

The winds of change are gathering momentum and much will transpire in the coming years. This will be globally scattered, not just America, and in these happenings many evacuations will take place as they always do in these occurrences. Whenever these occur you can know this. In local situations or large areas or blocks of land where disaster comes, it has been decided to take the children first. Beyond that the plans remain much the same as released in our book. We repeat, in any major disaster, some evacuation is taking place. They search in vain to find these many bodies for they have not remained, they have been lifted just before the occurrence takes place when they are seen to be in the pathway of its devastation. The figures released by the press are always inaccurate and not based on any real evidence of the true happenings. Our ships are always heavily gathered over these spots of trouble but are not visible to the average eye. For such would create more confusion on the scene if we were seen by all. As it is, we accomplish our purpose without interference with use of our beams and booster platforms. (Ashtar was speaker for this paragraph.)

ON EARTH ASSIGNMENT: THE COSMIC AWAKENING OF LIGHT WORKERS, WALK-INS AND ALL STAR-BORN REPRESENTATTIVES

Those who are ready for end time events still need to know the game plan. They need to know where to "get their tickets" and when the ships arrive. We want all who are ready to be lifted off this planet as soon as is possible. We do not wish to delay this process for it is a very big task.

There must first be a desire to go. In most cases a physical evacuation is involved, but in a few cases the light body will be ready to take the soul into the next dimension without using the ships. These do not need further truth, for they will have already taken on the Christ body which brings all knowingness. Those who need to depart by ship will gather in areas to which larger ships have access. This certainly means a departure from the cities; a move which many will not care for. They have roots which need much uplifting.

For those willing to depart there is no time better than now. They do not have to wait for the coming chaos to bring them into the Light. The sequence of events that are to follow will only be necessary for those who need this kind of event to bring them into the Light. They won't accept what is happening until the house around them crumbles. It must be remembered that the Father does not want any of His Children to be hurt. He only desires them to know Him, for without this knowing they will be unprepared FOR THE HIGHER REALMS. THE COMING EVENTS ARE DESIGNED TO BRING ABOUT AN AWARENESS OF THE FATHER. THIS IS TRULY THE ONLY MESSAGE THERE IS, and when the Mother Earth trembles, that IS the lesson!

The Kingdom of Heaven is already here, it only needs to be acknowledged. Before the heavens were cleared they were restricted by the dark forces. Now no obstacle remains for souls connecting with the higher realms. Christ is within all. It is not a matter of being converted but rather a process of one's acceptance of one's Divine Self. This is the message of hope to be introduced to the world. The soul goes through the experience of realizing the God Within.

Lessons from World Governments

The sum total of events to come before your scheduled coming inauguration will result in such political turmoil there is likely to be a reassessment of the entire process. There is the potential for such earth-shattering events before you, that the entire system will be altered. It comes through the combined effect of economic chaos and geological disorder. This is why we are bringing forth this stress upon Spiritual Lessons at this time. This must become one nation under God, and ONE WORLD UNDER GOD. This will be the direct result of the economic chaos.

The man-made plans for your coming elections holds many surprises. This includes the announcement of another candidate to appear on the scene if we are required to do this by oncoming events. Chaos will create last-minute confusion. God has ordained certain changes that require the anchoring of Light in individuals assigned to certain roles. The two individuals currently promoted for this responsibility do not have the consciousness required for the events that are scheduled for the world. One who comes in the Name of the Father is being prepared. We will provide a set of circumstances that will lead this one into his proper role. If all things come to pass that we now see are about to happen in the coming years, the entire election process could some day soon be thrown into disarray. When your Divinely appointed leader is ready, he will appear on the scene and all preparations will be made to assure his proper place in government of this nation.

The political scene is the result of a much larger problem in the consciousness of man. We are not interested in focusing on any present individual, but on the problems which need to be addressed in terms of lessons for the masses. America must learn that she is not capable of running the country she has been entrusted with without GOD!

America's remaining karma is a heavy one. She has been perpetrating her war consciousness into the minds of many other nations. This is being resolved by the Light workers who are transmuting this karma but there is always the possibility of retribution as has occurred in the Persian Gulf and through otherwise seemingly unrelated incidences of disasters. From the standpoint of earth Karma, the Persian Gulf incident is completely over. America experienced some earth Karma there but it was primarily written between the nations you now refer to as Iran and Iraq.

The Planetary Council of Twelve

(JUST A FEW DAYS PREVIOUS TO THE CONCLAVE FOR THIS HIERARCHICAL RELEASE, ASHTAR HAD GIVEN THESE WORDS THAT FOLLOW)

ON EARTH ASSIGNMENT: THE COSMIC AWAKENING OF LIGHT WORKERS, WALK-INS AND ALL STAR-BORN REPRESENTATTIVES

I am bringing into the dimension, several of my dependable officers to take up residence, who operate at the top level energies. I cannot say the length of their awakening time after the transfer is made, but their coming will be of immediate noticeable help to the entire program.

Our fleets have been exceedingly active with all of the additional detailed monitoring imposed on both the east coast and the Baha peninsula. We have been attempting to hold things steady but we are now limited in the holding we are permitted to engage. Our calculations indicate the west coast will see action the last of this year. The monitoring of people as they gather in crowds (a good time to do that) is not producing any cause for joy with us. There is much shallowness and human curiosity but little deep personal commitment. As events come into play, this could change rapidly.

(At the opening of this central conclave for seven days of communication through the Throne Energies a thrilling announcement was made.)

THE PLANETARY COUNCILS HAVE ARRIVED. THIS HAS JUST HAPPENED. WE HAVE BEEN MAKING PREPARATIONS FOR THEM AND THIS IS THE FIRST ANNOUNCEMENT OF THEIR ARRIVAL. The Stars have brought forth these interplanetary Beings into embodiment through the process of overshadowing Angels, with unique individuals in the sense that they will be completely GOD CONSCIOUSNESS. There will be no need for the "babysitting," like those in the current awakening process, for these are the pure essence of Love and Light.

The Planetary Council is an Elect Group of officials representing the Interplanetary Organizations who are responsible for bringing planet earth into total cooperation with her Cosmic neighbors. They are a group of Volunteers who were appointed by the High Masters of the Universe. They are one and the same as those energies who represent the Intergalactic Organizations but their energies are stepped down for this mission. We prefer not to use the term walkins, because it does not adequately vibrate with the full intensity of their Beings. These souls are very high in evolutionary standards, and will vibrate at a much higher frequency thereby creating the necessary opportunities to execute their purposes. We have overshadowed great world leaders in the past, but until this time our efforts have been restricted by the presence of the fallen ones.

It is intended that they will make their collective presence known to the government leaders as soon as the financial markets take their irreconcilable nosedive. This event will allow God thoughts to enter. Following the financial crash the Planetary Council appears on the scene but their presence will not yet be felt by the masses. The egos of current political leaders will arrange for a more subtle role for the Council during that time. Nevertheless, be it understood that the Planetary Council will act independently from any form of political leadership. The next President of the United States will be a high ranking official of the planetary realms who has been faced with the process of awakening. That is exactly the process that will be taken with all of the great angelic leaders on the planet at this time. This entity we hope to reveal during the extreme crisis period, will evidence the proper leadership skills to bring GOD CONSCIOUSNESS into the American System.

The World Peace Plan

Humanity must fully understand the lessons that are leading to all of the scheduled oncoming events. This includes the message of world peace. Man is finally beginning to learn that war is not the answer to anything. It is a part of the problem.

The United Nations is in a state of extreme disorder. There is not much there to salvage at the present time. Peace has begun to reign on this planet because of the Light Workers. This is the reason, contrary to the United Nations taking the credit. The United Nations will not be used for the purposes of the Planetary Council at all. They will endeavor to use some existing structure but all is to be brought down and what is to come will be of the new.

ONE OF THE THINGS THE PLANETARY COUNCIL MEMBERS ARE HERE TO ACCOMPLISH IS TO BRING FORTH THE WORLD PEACE PLAN. The world peace plan is important because it brings a recognition of the Brotherhood of Man! Man has failed to see his connection to the Almighty Creator. Man must first understand his connection to his fellow members of the specie before he can fully grasp the nature of his relationship to his God. It is not possible that mankind would have an opportunity to see that which he is, while his focus is on destroying the very nature of his Being.

ON EARTH ASSIGNMENT: THE COSMIC AWAKENING OF LIGHT WORKERS, WALK-INS AND ALL STAR-BORN REPRESENTATTIVES

This may take many forms, from disrespect for the body of the physical Being, to the destruction of those who do not conform to the standards set by man. The lesson of the peace plan is its method, which requires the attention of each soul upon the planet. NO longer can man look outside of himself for the answers. PEACE COMES FROM WITHIN. Through the divine interworking of the God Consciousness there will come about the Universal Peace Plan On Earth, and good will toward all men.

The Global Peace Plan is a model of the Universal Peace Plan that has always been projected from the Throne. This is sometimes referred to as the Brotherhood, or the Unity, or the Oneness. This will be the projection of this Universal Peace initiative. We call it Universal because some other planets are having to go through this final process as well.

On planet Earth there will be much resistance to the plan as many will ignorantly attach the project to the works of the AntiChrist. This represents another of the distortions of the book of Revelations as propagated by the fallen ones for their own ends. This will not be tolerated by the Lords of Light. We will be very firm in our presentation of this matter. The final earth war will be waged in the middle east. There will be much mocking of the Divine Plan by those who do not understand the Divine nature of those bringing forth the message. It will finally be understood why these martyrs (Rev. II) have to do what they do in order to get the attention of those who will not change without such a demonstration.

We are pleased to report that we have a majority of Light workers in the Soviet Union at this time. This has not always been the case, but it certainly is now and many are enjoying a higher state of consciousness at this time. These are very loving people who are willing to give their all to this greater presence they are aware of.

The United States has virtually all workers of the Light. This does not mean that they are awakened, of course, but it does indicate that the Light always gravitates to the highest level of energy. The Divine plan we have spoken of has in fact been overlayed on this region of the North American Continent, and there is an inner desire by those of the Light to come to this region.

The appearance of the Planetary Council will be within the Macro-Economic system of the planet, but not specifically through the normal political channels, as you call them. Their mission is Divine in nature and they will be given the opportunity to play by the Divine rules as opposed to the limitations of the rules of man.

Assorted Political Information

(A Question and Answer Session)

QUESTION: DO YOU HAVE ANY COSMIC CONTACT WITH THE LEADERS OF THE FORMER SOVIET UNION?

We most certainly do and they are consciously listening to us. It is a private matter. We communicate with them on a regular basis, as we also do with the American President and other more God-oriented souls.

QUESTION: WAS ABRAHAM LINCOLN AND JOHN F. KENNEDY THE STATE ENTITY?

President Lincoln would be considered an aspect of the Throne Energy. He and John E Kennedy were of the same soul composition. This does not mean that they were the same entity, for when the soul fragment returns to this earth plane, they can acquire greater awareness than just their fragment during a previous incarnation.

QUESTION: (Here we spoke of Robert Kennedy's frustration with the system.)

Yes, we can understand this. He will return to you outside the system shortly.

QUESTION: YOUNG JOE KENNEDY SEEMS TO BE ATTRACTING ATTENTION. DISCUSS HIM PLEASE.

He is indeed a part of the process which follows, but is not part of the Planetary Council. You sense his energy presence, as he is a part of our Divine projection on the planet. He is to be considered a high-ranking soul who is going to be able to come forth with his distinguished mission as soon as he completes his awakening.

ON EARTH ASSIGNMENT: THE COSMIC AWAKENING OF LIGHT WORKERS, WALK-INS AND ALL STAR-BORN REPRESENTATTIVES

QUESTION: WOULD YOU PLEASE DISCUSS OR EXPLAIN JUST WHAT IT IS ABOUT THE KENNEDY MEN THAT HAS SO MUCH CHARISMA AND MAGNETISM AS WELL AS LEADERSHIP ABILITIES?

The Kennedys represent a very powerful energy source from the Lord Michael Throne Energy. Persons with this blue ray of power identify with them well. They all have this power with the exception of those who have married into the family who actually often have difficulty with this powerful energy source. We have always been behind the Kennedy force as it represents my own Throne Energy. (Lord Michael was presiding over this question and answer session.)

QUESTION: WHAT ABOUT FRANKLIN DELANO ROOSEVELT?

He was an incarnation of one who is very high ranking in the Spiritual Hierarchy. He was chosen to introduce to mankind certain principles of loving and caring management of the system of governments. He has been with you in many incarnations usually in context with a government leader.

QUESTION: AND WINSTON CHURCHILL?

Winston Churchill was as well a high-ranking soul who was brought here for the specific purpose of bringing forth those principles of Love necessary in a world that would be war-torn.

QUESTION: THEN YOU OBVIOUSLY POSITIONED THESE TWO SOULS SPECIFICALLY FOR THEIR LEADERSHIP IN WORLD WAR II?

That is exactly correct. We were well aware that this great war of the world was going to take place. These among others were chosen to respond to the difficult nature of the coming events, just as there are those on the planet doing the same thing at this time.

WE WERE DISCUSSING JAPAN AND LORD ASHTAR CONTRIBUTED A PARAGRAPH:

Japan is doing fine in its outreach. They are experiencing sightings continually. They are studying and calling for our Fleets to come to them and also to guide them away from their islands to relocation. Many believe in this necessity and are attempting to provide a way for themselves. Many of the Japanese people who are gifted with the gift of communication with their ancestors have been receiving warnings to leave their islands when they can as soon as they can. Japan will be the first major disaster of that area of the world.

The Final Episode

The Divine blueprints are returning to the planet for its further evolving stages. This is the Divine imprint of the Divine codes which when impregnated into the planetary realm of third dimensional existence will bring the planet back into its original harmony with the universe. Remember, the planet has been under the influences of the fallen ones who have altered the Light codes that have been sent down from above. Whenever we would send the envelopes of Light with the Divine plans the fallen ones would interrupt them and change them enough to change the course of planetary evolution. These Light codes which are now coming forth are those which are necessary to bring the planet into its original evolutionary course.

Blue arcs of Light are now being seen that are passing overhead. These blue arcs are the positioning rods that are being used to re-align the planet into its correct orbital position for transformation into higher realms. These arcs also carry with them the Light which will release the Light workers from the forces of darkness in the earth plane. These arcs are what is known as Divine intervention in that they begin to penetrate all realms of matter and break up the dark energies that bind man to his world of limitation. You will see many changes in those who are of the Light, particularly those who are already doing God's work here on the planet. They will be freer in their approach to things and they will no longer be faced with the dark energies of the fallen ones.

The final cleansing of the planet will be that of fire which will be instigated by the return of the comet and the fallout from this event. It will not happen until the final days, but it will come about in short order. In your book of Revelations this comet is known as Wormwood and though much controversy will surround this subject it is in fact going to happen and must be filtered through the mass consciousness. Currently it has been identified as a mass in the sky. It is not the merkaba vehicle but the sighting of the great planet known by some as the 12th planet. This is in fact a great body of matter which John saw as a comet and referred to it as such. We will continue to call it a comet to be consistent but it matters not what it is called. It is going to collide with this planet and its impact will be quite devastating. Even though this will not be known for some time, it must be introduced to the masses. Those who have higher contact are encouraged to check out this information which will be given to any who ask for it.

This event of course remains as the final stand of the fallen ones and the final karmic cleansing necessary for the transformation process. This karmic cleansing has been partially averted, but the final days will have to witness the return of male energy that is necessary to balance the earth itself. This massive body of energy is due to reunite with the planet before the end of the final battle, so you can see that many of the fallen ones will not have the opportunity to complete their devastation on the planet. Had this been allowed to happen, the forces of Light would have to bear out the trauma; for now it is enough that the fallen ones will be unable to alter the course of this body of Light that is fast approaching the planet. They will sense the urgency in their plans to no avail. The planet must be joined with its Divine compliment which is scheduled to return in the latter part of the 1990's. By the year 2,000 the cleansing will have been completed. After this male energy is joined with the planet, after the comet's return, earth will enter into the electromagnetic null zone. In terms of electromagnetics, all must be in perfect balance, no polarities.

The Three and a Half Years of Revelations

The three and a half years as demonstrated in earth time are a literal translation of the Divine plan for these end times. However, it must not be interpreted as being in sequence of each other. We are not influencing you to speak anything other than truth. You have been taught this information in the higher realms and have been asked to stimulate these thoughts in others of the earth plane. The two three-and-a-half periods are just that. If we had wanted to express a seven year period we would have done so! But the three and-one-half year periods were known to have been holding specific events that could have been overlayed with whatever flexibility the Father needs during these latter days.

They have to hold that which has been prophesied but they do not need to be linear. They are in fact overlapping but not fixed in nature. The first three-and-a-half-year period is started, but it reflects more on the energies of God than on your calendar.

ON EARTH ASSIGNMENT: THE COSMIC AWAKENING OF LIGHT WORKERS, WALK-INS AND ALL STAR-BORN REPRESENTATTIVES

November of '87 is the date we want you to identify with in the sequence of events. To say that this was the start of the first three-and-a-half-year period would be correct; however, it is not enough to say that. There are greater concepts incorporated into these time frames. This was the date that the Israelis officially dictated a policy against those who were conflicting their plans for taking the Holy cities into their permanent control. This is the final point of control on the planet whereby the dark forces are able to carry out their part of the prophecy. This is a special control point that if it were to fall into the hands of the fallen ones, would create much difficulty for latter day events. This is why the two witnesses (Rev. II) eventually take their stand at this point. There will be war there, but not of the magnitude originally envisioned. The greatest threat of war focuses around the middle east, where religious factions continue to dominate the scene. This will continue as indicated. This turning of the tide is the last sequence of events that are portrayed in Revelations. We are indeed past the first three and-a-half year period now, but all that is included in this time sequence has taken effect. The final three-and-a-half-year period is already upon us. You would term this time condensing. The comet's arrival is very close and will occur before you realize it. This information comes to you from the highest source. All are encouraged to let these thoughts stimulate their own to seek further details, from their own reliable sources.

Our discussion of end-time events is enough to thoroughly prime thinking and trigger enthusiasm for the Divine program. Begin to think and talk of all of these things and seek more answers. This will create a wave upon which truth can come in, and communication with Masters on these matters, especially upon the Lessons that must be learned.

Armageddon and the Collective Messiah

Throughout these events there will be major resistance from the dark forces as well as those of the Light who have not been in the Light in this incarnation! They are the less evolved souls here strictly to evolve. They are not the volunteers. This distinction is necessary to understand. The dark ones are obvious, but these who are of the UNAWAKENED will be very difficult to handle. These will persecute the saints even unto death and rejoice when the messages cease to come. They will rejoice in knowing their ways can be preserved. Dark ones will stand back and watch this scenario knowing their days are numbered and that there is nothing, short of dying, that they can do. Through the ignorance of these earthly ones who

ON EARTH ASSIGNMENT: THE COSMIC AWAKENING OF
LIGHT WORKERS, WALK-INS AND ALL STAR-BORN REPRESENTATTIVES

are unable to respond to the messages of truth, the dark ones will mobilize themselves. This is when the harvest will come into full swing. Dark forces are easily identified, but those who walk the line of indecision will be delivered to other planetary bodies to continue to live in worlds of limitation until such time as they can process the truth. This group, which includes most of the planetary specie, will be evacuated before the final cleansing. Those who have awakened to the God within will continue on supporting the Father's plan until the final days, until their evacuation, and remain off the planet until reseeding time. At that time those ready to take on their Light bodies will do so. Those ready to ascend will also do so, but this is the way of the most highly evolved and few are capable of this.

You must all take care to keep your Light consciously, hourly consciously aware that you are Light, that every cell and atom of your body IS the Golden Light, consciously keeping this thought before you, consciously realize that you are part of the Light force that literally holds the planet together, consciously realize that you are indeed the salt of the earth. And if and when the salt shall be removed, the earth shall have lost its saviour. Thus all World Servers are highly accelerated at this time, greatly protected and endowed with an expansion of awareness and understanding.

The Light workers are all of those who have come here on assignment to planet earth. The "Collective Messiah" has already embodied through those souls who are here to hold the new blueprint for the planet, chosen ones, incarnated to hold that which is to come, while the Light workers address the current plan. The Collective Messiah has also been termed as the Legion of Special Volunteers. The Elect are all of those who have come in the name of Light to uplift this planet into a higher state of consciousness during these many eons of planetary history. The days have already been shortened, with the issue of war alone. Now we will see how the LIGHT WORKERS RESPOND to these other issues needing their attention. It is their efforts which have shortened the days.

The plan calls for the complete alliance with the Spiritual Body of Christ, who is the Collective Messiah now organized upon the planet. These have been chosen by their willingness to anchor the Light during these final end times. Not to be construed as only the Light workers, but rather a very special group of very responsible souls who represent the Christ Consciousness of the planet. They have been duly formed into a collective, which is anchoring the Light in this third dimensional realm.

Life's Highest Comfort

Divine Presence

Chapter 6

No Second Causes

"In the center of the circle

of the will of God ... I stand,

There can come no second causes

All must come from His Dear Hand."

Although humanity be buffeted by the storms raging through this world of duality and pain, there is within each soul the power to meet these storms with understanding, with courage, and with faith; and meeting them to rise from the darkness of unconscious instinct to the Light of conscious enlightened intelligence.

Like the wheel of fortune on a current television game, only one card is turned up at a time. Not a word, just a letter. So it is in our personal pursuit of revelation, one little clue at a time. Until finally that moment comes, like a starburst within our heart, clues begin to cluster together and form a traceable pattern. Maybe small but complete enough to our consciousness, and so the Great Adventure begins, to know thyself, to know thy God. The wonder of it all is that earth life with its endless mundane occupations could occupy us at all, but we have our purposes to fulfill so that the soul will find its way back to its home after having completed but a moment of the school of earth life, to go on to greater things.

ON EARTH ASSIGNMENT: THE COSMIC AWAKENING OF LIGHT WORKERS, WALK-INS AND ALL STAR-BORN REPRESENTATTIVES

The I AM PRESENCE spoke to me one day on the Orbit of the Soul:

"Orbits of souls are like unto orbits of worlds. There is a pathway ordained, a route to follow which comes from the nature of things as kept in motion by the Source of all motion and life. A soul comes forth from the Source and is placed into a chosen orbit. It proceeds upon the Pathway with consistency and constancy if it is held within the will of the Father by its own unity and integration of that will.

"If there is a digression from its pathway or orbit, due to self-will rising in opposition to its natural pathway, then it is drawn by the magnetism of self-will from its orbit into an opposite direction.

"Many lifetimes may come and go, until finally that soul is drawn magnetically back to its own Pathway by a renewed desire to seek unison with the Source and the Father's will for its destiny.

"By virtue of being within its orbit again, great momentum, power, and dormant abilities are once more accelerated and applied to the environment of that Pathway.

"Then all that was laid aside, or placed inactive, begins once again where momentum was denied, as the soul returns to its original destiny. The fewer the times of digression, the fewer the sojourns through the school of earth. Learning stands side by side with serving. All are in the school of earth, even those who come to -serve. Divine processes ever increasing the frequency within the orbit draws the soul inexorably into the bosom of its Source.

"When within the orbital Pathway, consciously, willingly, it is a natural thing to anticipate that all of the principles that have come forth from the Source, all of the Laws of Being and Doing will be at the disposal of the orbiting soul for all of its needs and deeds. An acknowledgment of the Source, an understanding of the Laws of Being, and the Principles of Creation, can be applied to bring any manifestation into a soul who orbits within the Father's will.

"Do not underestimate yourselves as sons and daughters of

ON EARTH ASSIGNMENT: THE COSMIC AWAKENING OF LIGHT WORKERS, WALK-INS AND ALL STAR-BORN REPRESENTATTIVES

God, but grasp, yea demand, the infilling, the flowing of Divine Force throughout your Being, your lifestream, to expand your ability, to push you forward in action, pulling others into the vacuum you leave behind. Think of yourselves as magnets, as pulsating magnetic force; feel it flowing through you and then passing out to the environment that surrounds you. In this way the world is energized with Divine energies wherever your feet shall tread. You are the embodied positive-negative principle of the Source, manifesting as that Source which will change the minds of people and change the world, if they will have it so. If they will not, we can only withdraw.

I AM THAT I AM opens to thee rivers of Force to flow within thee and out of this creation."

Evolving Toward Perfection

At the time of the first descent into a lesser spirit form, the early inhabitants of earth's mists were only denser of spirit, not of physical form. The creation of density came much later. In those beginnings spirit walked the land in total communion with the realms above. Then followed long periods of the attempt of self to assert itself. The symbology of the forbidden fruit, and the eating of the apple, represented the entrance of freedom of will into man's domain. Henceforth the innocence and the carefreeness of man was taken over by self efforts at survival and self-created hardships of life. At first some fellowship with spirit beings still remained, but in due time all such was cut off by man's own density and thus man was ejected from his beautiful garden by his own will.

Since that time cycle, many higher beings on volunteer assignment to earth, have taken upon themselves entrance into the human kingdom in order to assist mankind to extricate themselves from this descent into density and its resulting karma. These heavenly souls have likewise of necessity exposed themselves to the earth's limitations and attracted karma to themselves as well. Thus the two sets of souls have evolved together side-by-side, until the end of time, when all of earth's karma shall be balanced by the latter group and some for the former.

The Beloved Teacher taught that the truth of the God Within would set us free. This glorious sense of Beingness and Freedom means to be free of the need to defend ourselves and others; to be free of the feeling of being threatened by others; to be free of the need of power and control over others; to be free from allowing others to manipulate and control us; to be free from doubt and uncertainty; to be free of the need to impress and be impressed by others; to be free of the need to hide who we really are ... magnificent Beings of Light who elected to take on the human condition to bring Harmony to earth. The Lords of Light who gave the material earlier in this book speak again:

"There are times when the truth is reflected in people, but they are unable to complete their assignments because of the soul's desire to take one last stab at experiencing its own will. The soul knows that the truth rests in the Divine state, but it still seeks out the mysteries of life through the process and trial and error. This may be seen in those who seek out our teachings but are unwilling to make a commitment to God. This commitment cannot be forced, because the soul will always reject that which is not born of its own desire. When the desire to serve God is foremost in the mind, then the action to serve will follow.

"Although many are awakening there is still a reluctance to fully commit to the Father. The ways of the past are so strong they cannot get free from the lower self to take on the Divine self. Too many reach a plateau but are unable to advance to the next level, without an extra push from those whose work it is to lead them inward to their God Consciousness."

Check Baggage Here

The sense of urgency that comes across when the Lords of Light speak leave no doubt that humanity must get its act together and prepare for coming events:

"All must get their temples in order to make the transition. This involves a total letting go of all that is holding them to the past, and to their expectations of the future. Too many will want to hang onto their old baggage and this simply is not possible, if man is going to get ready to leave this platform he must make himself ready for the journey which involves the complete letting go of EVERYTHING! There is not enough time left to sort out what is good or bad. Be willing to completely surrender to the Divine self. Those unwilling to do this will be unable to make the leap into the next dimension of reality. This will be an inexplicable time for many who face the instantaneous removal of one into the higher realm while the other remains in place, not conscious of what has just happened. You can see that confusion will be the rule of the day. None of us have seen such an event carried out in this way. Normally an entire planetary body is ready to take the leap in consciousness together, for in the other realms they have not had to face the separation of the fallen ones. This has only occurred on- a few planets and earth is by far the largest such project of its kind. It has not come without a lot of stress to the planetary body, but it will not be long before she is freed from all of this contamination."

What kind of Universe would it be around here if there were not any laws and Universal principles to glue it all together? All incarnations are strung together as one long continuing life. The rewards are equal to the service rendered. WE cannot outrun God's Law or short circuit it, or get away with anything; there's no free lunch. Life is a do-it-yourself project and what we invest or put into it is what we get. There seems to be a general consensus that, "...If at first you don't succeed, fix the blame!" The old baggage of blaming God, blaming parents, blaming society, blaming circumstances or whoever or whatever, has to be checked here. We're in the driver's seat and we can take the credit for what we turned out to be, because life is a do-it-yourself project. WE can no longer hide behind the hypocrites or the churches or any other such thing. We must now stand up and accept responsibility for our lives, and our choices. WHAT WE HOLD IN OUR CONSCIOUSNESS MANIFESTS IN OUR LIVES. As we think so shall it be. Consciousness needs to be changed and needs to be prepared to accept personal accountability and the truth that God is in everything. His lessons are everywhere.

As I prepared this material, there was another intense tragedy as a jet airliner crashed just off the runway of a Texas airport splitting the craft right through the middle. Perhaps 30 lost their lives in the view of the other 80 or so who survived. I asked the Lords of Light to discuss the spiritual lesson involved. They replied:

"The souls who perished in that crash have given their lives to serve as a warning to their observers and the masses, to always place their lives and the details of their traveling into the Father's hands every trip that must be made. These souls witness that nothing may be taken for granted in this dimension apart from the Grace and Love of the Father Creator. The very breath that is given is a gift from the Father. Regardless of the physical cause for the splitting of the craft, the dominant truth is that these souls were chosen to be lifted through this means as a warning exercise to the rest of the world that the Father must be involved in every step of life's journey and undertaken by placing all details of His Loving Care. This is the lesson that must be learned when tragedy comes. But to those souls who elected for this work, it is not a tragedy. It is a martyrdom for the Father."

I used to weary in the jelly-making process, having to stand there continually spooning off all the gook that would keep coming to the surface as the mixture boiled. But I was also very proud of the clear, colorful result as it was stored in its shiny clean jars. Our Father is more patient with us than I was with my jelly. He is willing to take as long as you choose, but He will keep the fire going until the process is finished. But our Father is not making jelly, He is refining pure gold. Refined gold is pure gold, no other elements are present. The Father continues to remove the dross as it comes to the surface until the gold reflects His image, then His process is complete. In our lives He will enter on some inward attitude, some trait of lovelessness, some negative root of bitterness, some lack in our relationship with Him, until finally that dross of negativity is brought up for transmutation. It is then we recognize it or what it is and we seek His help for its removal. Thus continually, as various aspects of our inner being are brought to the surface for us to acknowledge as ours alone, His love clears it all away. Rejoice when your worst or less admirable traits are "up for transmutation," for the refiner is bringing forth His pure gold, and you are getting rid of a lot of excess baggage. The chakra's will pulsate, the energy will flow and push against the blockage clutched for so long. Do not look too much to yourself or analyze within too much, but look to our God, who is a consuming fire.

The Elohim speak:

"We, the Elohim, are concerned about the individual progress as well as with the progressive evolution of the entire Universe. No form of Creation is to be left without support from the many interdimensional realms. You have been sheltered from the TRUTH for far too long. Now is the time to acknowledge your presence in the Universal order. You are Beings of Light taken form in the physical dimension to experience that which is necessary for Universal order. You have chosen this experience on planet earth to enable you to grow in the LIGHT. Stagnation has no place; nor does devolution, when the mind, body and soul of man reverts to thought patterns of old. This is the reason for the state of things on the planet at this time. Man is no longer able to be guided and directed by the Universal Mind but instead is entrenched in thought patterns of past origin which were used in the past to learn the lessons of that stage of growth. Having failed to recognize the lessons man is continually faced with, reorientating himself to similar circumstances to achieve further progress. Once man accepts the lessons THAT HE HIMSELF HAS IMPOSED for growth, he can then be free." (Obid-Channel)

The Attitude Syndrome

I learned long ago that there are many things in this world that matter very little, and most things matter nothing at all. But before that, such little things seemed to matter so much. When I was a child of about fourth grade level, my shoes had totally destructed, even beyond the stage of my mother inserting any more cardboard in the soles where the holes were. Without money to buy more at the time, she concluded I would have to wear hers to school. Admittedly I was a big girl for my age, but not that big. I submissively donned the despised footwear and went out slamming the apartment door. I immediately went up to the roof and stayed there all day until I saw the school flag lowered, a few blocks away. I made my timely entrance back at our apartment very pleased with my subterfuge, as hungry and thirsty as it was possible to be. No sacrifice was too great for my pride in its refusal to be seen in those shoes. But, I was only a child.

Many decades later, I was busy painting the Deming farmhouse when a necessary trip to the town post office was suddenly remembered. Quickly I donned a presentable garment and created my own dust storm driving out the long lane. As I rushed into the post office to join the long line, looked down at my feet and noticed the old paint loafers adorned with an abundance of spots of many colors; a bit discordant with the pretty suit I was wearing. But now I was grown up. My footwear didn't bother me at all, the long line of people notwithstanding. Because, you see, I knew at home I had two lovely new pairs of shoes and these did not represent all that I had. I KNEW I HAD SOMETHING BETTER WHEN I GOT HOME! Hasn't it been that way many times in life, when you have been ill-used or mistreated or brought to tears or falsely accused or harshly misjudged, or deprived of many things; hasn't it been that you could possess your soul in peace and stillness within, because you knew that someday when you got back home, the Father would have something for you far better! WHEN YOU COME TO KNOW THAT THIS LIFE IS NOT ALL THERE IS ... THAT BEYOND IS SOMETHING FAR BETTER, AND IN PATIENCE YOU WILL WAIT, then that is truly the peace that passeth all understanding.

ON EARTH ASSIGNMENT: THE COSMIC AWAKENING OF
LIGHT WORKERS, WALK-INS AND ALL STAR-BORN REPRESENTATTIVES

It is easy to change a difficult situation. You can change yourself by changing your attitude to that situation. It has been said that nothing that happens to us is as important as our attitude to that which has happened to us. And the attitudes of life are the Father's testing grounds. Everyone is intrinsically good. It is only their behavior that bothers us, not the person. We can love the person.

My children had a crib toy which taught me a great lesson. It was a doll with a lovely smile on its face and joyful expression. It had a rounded and weighted base so that no matter how much you slapped it around or threw it aside, it always returned to its upright smiling position ready for more. I thought as I watched it, "So what if life knocks me down once in a while ... I know where I've come from, I know why I'm here and I know where I'm going. And I know someday I'll return home to something better." They once called this "blessed assurance." Now it's called "total awareness." What's in a name? It's having it that matters.

Let us suppose, dear friend, that you went to the mailbox one morning and discovered you had received a million dollar check in the mail. Blood pressure would pound in your arteries, your heart would palpitate like a motor boat, your face would flush red, your eyes would sparkle. You would scream, you would wave the check in the air, you would jump up and down and in general go into a kind of emotional bliss; a real FEELINGS SPREE. But none of these things would be what made you a millionaire. Actually you could sit there like a dullard, a lifeless clod, totally stunned in a daze, a dead pan face. But it would be the check in your hand that made you a millionaire. NOT YOUR FEELINGS, NOT YOUR HIGHS, NOT YOUR LOWS, NOT YOUR PHYSICAL EXUBERANCE OR THE DEPTH OF YOUR LUNGS. It would be the check that determined your status. So you see, as long as you have a check in your hand signed by the Heavenly Father and paid to the order of your name, it's the statement that makes you His Child, no matter what your feelings may say at any time.

Spiritual experiences do bring bliss. Jesus analyzed the Kingdom of God as being two thirds emotion, righteousness, peace and joy. RIGHTEOUSNESS means right thinking, right attitudes.

Righteousness is a state of Being, it is not a feeling. But righteousness does produce joy and Peace and they are emotions. Feelings can

ON EARTH ASSIGNMENT: THE COSMIC AWAKENING OF
LIGHT WORKERS, WALK-INS AND ALL STAR-BORN REPRESENTATTIVES

fluctuate with the moon, the body, and circumstances, even biorhythm. But the Presence of the Father-Mother God within is infallible. I AM THAT I AM, the God within!

You want the Bread of Truth. I do not want to give you a stone. I give you truth. You are Sons and Daughters of the Most High. You are Kings and Priests of the Lord's Hosts. You are members of an aristocratic family. You have come from the far off vistas's of other worlds. You have come prepared for warfare. You have come to lay down your physical lives if need be. REMEMBER WHO YOU ARE. WALK INVINCIBLE AS THE ANGELS OF GOD THAT YOU ARE. Awaken the sleeping giant within you....

"Thou must be true thyself

If thou the truth would teach;

Thy heart must overflow

If you another soul would reach."

We reach others out of our own overflow. A few drops overflowing to a thirsty soul will not diminish me if my own barrel is full and running over. I am attempting to say something very important to you here. Please follow me. It is a wonderful, indescribable thing, after you have spent a lifetime in a spiritual desert, thirsting for Love, Wisdom, and Understanding most of that life, then to suddenly find God within, and your little thimble running over; it is indeed a wonderful thing.

You want to run out; start a group, perchance a lecture tour, but God doesn't open any of these doors. You become almost obnoxious in your zeal. Like the young one, squealing in his crib, "Hey everybody, I'm alive!" But the world goes by, waiting for him to grow up. Or like the youth in a gleam of inspiration and knowingness announces, "I am going to be a neurosurgeon!" But he is a long way from holding the scalpel in his hot palm. God does not ignore your thimble full. But He knows that in your future, "...there is a river that shall make glad the people of God," and there you might give them to a drink out of your overflow. GOD CONSCIOUSNESS IS THAT MIGHTY RIVER!

Volunteers, do not be afraid to let the Father go before you.

ON EARTH ASSIGNMENT: THE COSMIC AWAKENING OF LIGHT WORKERS, WALK-INS AND ALL STAR-BORN REPRESENTATTIVES

Doors will open like the supermarket doors, wherever the souls of your feet tread. To get something to the world, you must yourself get the thing many times multiplied, lest the winds of the fallen ones blow you aside. A Lighthouse must have a large and firm foundation to stand firm in the billows roll. Don't attempt to be a bountiful with too puny a supply.

The Flow of Truth

I have been instructed by both the Elders and the Extraterrestrials to address the problem of division within the Family of God upon the planet. With their promised help, I shall do this. Perhaps you are wondering, "Which Family!" Any family! "Which church?" Any church!" "Which movement?" Any movement!

I want to show you why we have divisions. I hope to present the flow of truth to your understanding in a simple way. I want to express the dangers of crystallization. I hope that you will see where we are today in the progressiveness of revelation.

There was a time when it was recommended that to humble oneself before the Creator, one would grovel in the ground or throw dust in the head. Now it is a different time. Now we need to think.

Many statements hitherto veiled in mysticism and mythology can now be related to the technology of our day. We must open our minds and become aware. Becoming aware means realizing how much more there is for you to know. Dogmatic bigotry is passé. To attain some minute position and vociferously claim from that moment of time, all revelation has now ceased, results in the very blind deceiving the very blind. No one has all there is! What they have is a fragment of awareness of how much more there is to discover, to learn, to experience. The moment the ink dries on a written creed, it becomes an anachronism. We move on a great escalating stairway of Awareness, with always some behind us, some before us. Whatever we knew before we came, is behind the veil that was dropped upon us, once again it must all be pulled through our human consciousness. That requires obedience, consistency, stickability, humility. At every step of the way of accomplished awareness, the dweller on the threshold is there, ready to pat you on the back and say, "Look what you know now. You should stop now and stay here. "

ON EARTH ASSIGNMENT: THE COSMIC AWAKENING OF LIGHT WORKERS, WALK-INS AND ALL STAR-BORN REPRESENTATTIVES

We are spiritual Beings going through physical experience for our own growth! Just like you, when I was triggered to higher understanding, I devoured all the books and walked in and out of system after system, noticing as I did so, the competitiveness, the critical energies, the volumes of contradictory material all contributing to the confusion. Lady Master Athena kindly came to my rescue with this very practical message on the "Progressiveness of Revelation":

"It is necessary that we permit the disciple to broaden awareness of that which is projected and has been projected to mass consciousness. This permits us to build a background of that which has been given in the presentation of truth. This is the progressive release of Light.

"When a great channel of Light is found, and one in which the Hierarchy has confidence, it takes much gentleness and reasoning to pull them away from the old religious thought forms that have been built. Due to the age and durability of the conception, this is sometimes quite difficult. It may necessitate a new lifestream for the purpose.

"The newer revelations, or shall we say presentations of the ancient wisdom, are in most cases a purer form, since they have not yet crystallized or fossilized into a given status quo. But where new insight is released, it usually cannot penetrate the existing crystallizations. Consequently, there will be new ways and new systems of presentations brought forth as the time of the eclipse of the ages approaches.

"When truth is released in this way, it always carries a genesis of Abundant Life and flow. Indeed, you 'feel the Spirit.' For this reason, it is ultimately better to look upward and not backward in your search. Remember the words of the Great Master. 'You cannot put new wine into old wineskins.' True, one must become aware of that which has gone before in the philosophical pursuit, but it is always well to keep one's ear attuned to heaven as one reads.

"Do not hurry to accept the closed conclusions of other closed minds. Minds may find just so much and rejoice and press their new Light to their bosom, and then close the door. But the works they do become necessary for souls not yet aspired to their level of attainment.

"Hostility arises, when another, of deeper insight, attempts to

ON EARTH ASSIGNMENT: THE COSMIC AWAKENING OF LIGHT WORKERS, WALK-INS AND ALL STAR-BORN REPRESENTATTIVES

lead these aspirants higher. There are no exceptions to this rule, for Truth marches on and waits for no man. The progressive release of Light is ordained, individually and cosmically.

"You have with you Walk-Ins and Earth Volunteers. These many, now entering, will be instruments in raising the planetary vibrations to levels undreamed of in the present occult community. But you will still have those in the old thought forms who have refused to progress with the Plans of the Hierarchy. Now what can we say of these?

"First, their usefulness has fulfilled its day. In many cases, revelation is now bypassing many of the old progressive steps, and placing the old aspirant directly on the threshold of initiation.

Second, they have forfeited the opportunity to be partakers of the harvest of new souls who now enter and their fruits begin to shrivel on the vine.

"Third, deterioration and a slow death will finally weed out these older crystallizations by the sheer Abundant Growing Force and Vitality of the new forces. So it is, as the Great Master hath spoken, 'Let both remain, side by side, until the harvest.'

"Find and study all of the best that there is, but be not overtaken by their crystallizations pattern. Instead, flow freely, with the Holy Spirit, knowing that a bit of heaven is in them all but the best is yet to come. I Am Athena Your Sister in the Ascension."

Man's Response to Revelation

It is written that the superstition of the past is the science of the present, the proverb of the future, absorbed into accepted mental life. An arbitrary refusal of new Light seems to be just as superstitious as a blind acceptance. Within the history of all progress, it is always met with extraordinary initial opposition.

Souls experience spiritual awakening usually, one at a time, not by households, not by family. Thus Truth, in all situations can become the source of division, making "...a man's enemies those of his own household, of his church, or his contemporaries. Man responds to spiritual quickening on four different levels. Therefore humanity of all ages has always had these four pathways of approach, all leading upward, one into another. The pathway is a very long one, long enough to include every soul, for everyone is on the pathway, somewhere.

As soon as one experiences the inner splendor of the Christ Within, one soon experiences the revelation of the Christ within All Others, in every eye, behind every face. Though they do not know this themselves, the enlightened one sees them even if they think they are lost. For each soul alive in the Universe of Light, where Light created Life and sustains it, Light is everywhere present. (On the page following this one you will find an organized diagram of facts describing the four responses of humanity to spiritual revelation. At this point in study it would be advisable to read it carefully, slowly, and absorb the distinctions that are listed under each pathway. Please do this.)

As surely as if you were beholding a narrow path through the woods, expanding until it becomes a six lane super highway, so also can you perceive within this information the progressive expansion of humanity's response to God since earliest medieval times. One thinks of the bloody religious Crusades, the combined rule of Church and Monarchy, the hordes of mad bigotry, the ecclesiastical tribunals through which humanity has come. Yet with these also, the mountain peaks stand out of holy lives lived in their midst down through recorded history; the evidence of parallel pathways simultaneously. And so it is today.

The great religions of the world may all be positioned somewhere within the diagram. You will recognize the church of your childhood, the progression of your unfoldment, the attainment of this hour. Could you delve deeper into the soul background of your religious concepts in the life before this one, and the one before that, ad infinitum, you would perceive your soul following along these outlined pathways, an enlightenment unfolded your continuing pathway. The initial quickening of this lifetime, picks up the golden thread where it was dropped at your transition, and you face the responsibility of going on, growing, advancing, from initiation to initiation in this embodiment.

Thus as you study the progression of man's response, it can readily be seen that all men are somewhere upon the pathway. Therefore, there is no valid reason for contempt of lovelessness toward the spiritual understanding or concept of another soul. Neither is there any validity for pride of our own. For all have come up through the same school; the lessons of earthly embodiment that have resulted in our growth and spiritual progression from glory unto glory.

We are at this moment the sum total of all that we have ever seen, all that we have ever believed or experienced. This is where we are, and as so often observed, we reveal where we are when we open our mouth."

There is therefore no integrity, no justification, no goal in participating in or supporting or proselytizing any energy focus that is advocating the separation, or cutting off, of any other body of sons and daughters of God! When this great lesson is absorbed by mankind, and the love it fosters is released to permeate the atmosphere of this planetary body, then our world will have experienced its ascension to its destiny. The Law of the One, the Oneness of all creation, this is the essential message taught by the entire Spiritual Hierarchy and the Extraterrestrial messages from other worlds. Where there is complete dedication to Light upon the planet (-Thy Kingdom Come"), the pounding white water of Universal Love of the Hosts of Heaven will beat against the rocks of past mistakes; the enthronement of self, pushing, sweeping forward in torrential cleansing leaving them all behind. THE MIGHTY RIVER OF THE UNFETTERED I AM THAT I AM, THE GOD WITHIN, hidden splendor, washes away the old thought patterns that divide the sons and daughters of God.

The Almighty hid Himself to the last place that men would look, within their own Being. But when man finds the Mighty God Within, he can claim his Divinity as Kings and Priests unto God! Be careful not to be carried away or throw the chest out too far if someone says that you were once a King or once a Priest, so what! You need to know what you are, where you are right now. And where you are right now should not compare to where you were ten years ago, ten months ago, even ten weeks ago; Light is moving so fast. On the stage of entertainment, the round focus of Light has to diligently keep pace with the entertainer as he moves from spot to spot across the stage, but in our spiritual world the reverse is the case. We must strive constantly to keep pace with the LIGHT AS IT MOVES FORWARD ON OUR PATHWAY, less we be left behind in our lethargy, or television addiction, or pursuits of the lower self, or whatever diversion dulls our spiritual aspirations.

ON EARTH ASSIGNMENT: THE COSMIC AWAKENING OF LIGHT WORKERS, WALK-INS AND ALL STAR-BORN REPRESENTATTIVES

We Are One

The Great Master taught that we are the branches, and He is the Vine, and the branches cannot bear fruit of themselves except they abide in the Vine. To oversimplify a profound truth, may we consider that it is as if the Supreme Being, All That Is, said, "I must get down to that place before it explodes." And so it was that the Supreme Creator deliberately divided itself, into billions of little drops of Being, like billions of drops of rain descending from one tremendous cloud. The billions of drops of Being came to this Space to clean it up, and my friend, it will be cleaned up!

Some time ago, I dropped a thermometer on the floor. The strip of thin glass shattered and the mercury within separated into a mass of tiniest beads that rolled out in all directions, independently. I followed them and began to nudge them toward each other. They would find each other through their own inherent magnetism. As they found another and another, eventually with my push and encouragement they came to a cluster and all fused easily back into one.

Only our human personalities of the lower self are individualized, polarized and unique in a beautiful way. Our I AM THAT I AM, THE GOD WITHIN, THE CHRISTED BEING HAS NO DISUNITY, IT IS ALL HARMONY. For That within you is the Divine Nature ... It is the Real You. It is creatively impossible to spawn disunity when working from within.

To create disharmony, which brings separation, we must go outward to the surface periphery and work from the outer level of self and human personality. To dissolve disharmony in any situation we must go within and work from the Christ Presence level. From there, failure is impossible since the God within is all harmony.

The Stone of Intolerance

Wherever upon the Pathway, it may be confronted, the intolerance of God's children one for another proceeds forth from the hardness of the "stony heart." In the prophecy of Ezekiel 36:26, the promise is given.

"Then will I sprinkle clean water (truth) upon you, and ye shall be clean. A new heart also will I give you, and a new spirit (God Consciousness) will I put within you, and I will take away the stony (intolerant, proud) heart."

ON EARTH ASSIGNMENT: THE COSMIC AWAKENING OF LIGHT WORKERS, WALK-INS AND ALL STAR-BORN REPRESENTATTIVES

That stone is not only intolerance, it is a closed mind.

In the 29th chapter of Genesis, there is a symbolical passage of scripture which has always moved me deeply. The scene is set at Haran's well, where shepherds are gathered with their flocks to water them. But a huge stone covered the mouth of the well, and the flocks were kept waiting until all the flocks were together, then with their combined push against it, it was rolled aside and the flocks had water. That stone was the barrier. Jacob came strolling by on his way to find Rachael, his betrothed. Noticing the flocks gathered around, he told Laban's men to water the sheep. They responded, "We cannot (water them) until all of the flocks be gathered together (unity, cooperation) till they roll away the stone (intolerance)."

Because it took the cooperation of them all together against the stone to have access (removal of barrier) to the water (truth). But in the time when the Bridegroom (Jacob) came for his bride (Rachael), be rolled the stone away and the flocks were watered.

WE CANNOT WATER THE FLOCKS OF GOD BECAUSE THE STONE OF INTOLERANCE IS IN THE WAY!

That stone also represents crystallization upon a point on the pathway, or fossilization as my own Teachers describe it. At any point in this condition within a group dynamic, new water (truth) cannot flow to the people of God.

We cannot remove the stone alone. Only the help of the God Within, the Christed Consciousness can do this. The Bridegroom United with His Bride can do it. The opening of the god Consciousness brings Oneness, Brokenness, Unity, to all of God's Children. This experience is the Big Combined Push from all of us, that will birth forth the final pang of the New Age.

WE ARE ONE, WE MUST ACT LIKE IT. WE MUST HARNESS OUR STRENGTH AS A MIGHTY ARMY OF LIGHTED BEINGS.

"And l, John, saw the Holy City, New Jerusalem, COMING DOWN FROM HEAVEN, prepared as A BRIDE ADORNED FOR HER HUSBAND. And I heard a great voice out of heaven, saying, BEHOLD THE TABERNACLE OF GOD IS WITH MEN, AND HE WILL DWELL WITH THEM, AND

THEY SHALL BE HIS PEOPLE, AND GOD HIMSELF SHALL BE WITH THEM AND BE THEIR GOD.

"And God shall wipe away all tears from their eyes; and there shall be no more death, neither sorrow, nor crying, neither shall there be any more pain, for the former things are passed away. I will give unto him that is athirst of the water of life freely." (Revelation 21:1-6)

And finally:

"And the Spirit and the Bride say, Come. And LET him that hearest say come. And LET him that is athirst Come. And WHOSOEVER WILL, LET HIM take of the WATERS OF LIFE (Truth) freely. "

Beloved, beautiful, loving, concerned, burdened Shepherds of the Flocks of God; dedicated, sincere, devoted Teachers of the Flocks of God, the Spirit says, "LET THEM ... take of the Water!" Get your heads out of the way, shift your hearts into Love-gear, and LET THEM who seek it, find their Truth, without condemnation, though it may be beyond yours. Yes, you are needed where you are, and there you remain until released, but those who must move-on to deeper waters, bless them and LET THEM go, and thus show forth your own Mastery. For the Good Shepherd leadeth his sheep beside the still waters.

The God Within

In the ecstacy of Thy Presence there is nothing but LOVE whether I look above me, or whether I gaze beneath me, or whether I draw to the right, or I'm drawn to the left, there is naught but LOVE.

I AM locked into a sea of DIVINE LOVE. As the tiniest fish glides its way In the depths of the ocean, So am I surrounded by His LOVE.

I realize there is nothing can touch me. That LOVE has not allowed. There is no pain so great That LOVE cannot bear it; There is no fiery heat, But that LOVE can hear its flame.

I AM only Thee. I care naught for anything; Any result, any accomplishment, Any reward, any self glory, For Thou art surrounding me.

**ON EARTH ASSIGNMENT: THE COSMIC AWAKENING OF
LIGHT WORKERS, WALK-INS AND ALL STAR-BORN REPRESENTATTIVES**

If souls are drawn in my direction, It is only because they see Thee. Thou are the magnet That draws them to Thyself. So be it LORD GOD unto Thee All things are Thine And I Am Thine and Thou art mine.

It can never be otherwise, For my being is forever in Thy care.

Thou within me remains Invincible, Unconquerable, Unlimited and Victorious. Incapable of loss to Thyself, No error nor mistake.

This is the power of all life,
All Mind, All Energy and All Creation.
And, let it be.
I Am lost in the bliss of my Peace with Thee,
There is nothing but Thee,
THE GOD WITHIN.

By Tuella

ON EARTH ASSIGNMENT: THE COSMIC AWAKENING OF LIGHT WORKERS, WALK-INS AND ALL STAR-BORN REPRESENTATTIVES

Life's Highest Reward

The Divine "Well done!"

Chapter 7

The Magnitude of the Mission

In a period of reverie a few days ago, I reflected upon the tremendous scope of the mission to this little planet; reviewing centuries of effort that have passed. In great heaviness I voiced my thought, "...it will all soon be over!" Then I clearly heard from within my room, applause from a few pair of hands, three or four perhaps. Then a few more hands joined in, then more from above the house, then many more above increasing in volume. Then beyond that reaching into the heavens the echoing of additional, gentle but swelling applause, until on and on it went, and I began to realize from the veritable thunder of the sound from every last corner of the Hierarchical Planes the heavens roared with the resounding ovation of the joy throughout Creation that, "...it will soon be over!" I wept and rejoiced with all of them. I heard a powerful voice say,

"So it is that all of this combined effort on behalf of this planet, through countless eons and eras, ere soon, the mission to Terra will be completed. And you shall have had a part in it repeatedly, again and again. Now you come to that last final episode with Our Presence beside you for that which must come."

A few years ago, one called Xylatra, one of the Ancient of Days, came to me to discuss earth's problems:

"It was in the beginning of all things that we came, when Creation was new and beauty was upon the planet. We came to populate and

ON EARTH ASSIGNMENT: THE COSMIC AWAKENING OF LIGHT WORKERS, WALK-INS AND ALL STAR-BORN REPRESENTATTIVES

propagate life in this new world. We brought Life and Wisdom and Teachings. We planted the seed of a new race, and watched its expansion into creatures of Light. We planted the animal kingdom and the winged creatures and covered the planet with flowers of all colors.

"Then it was that a great and terrible happening came upon this root race as the effects of the planetary sun began to deteriorate mind. Detrimental erosion took place in the mental bodies of those we planted, and faces, forms and figures changed, and they brought forth that which we had not planted and became alienated in spirit and desire from Our Presence.

"We were forced out and away, pushed beyond, by the great clouds of negativity that arose and covered the planet. Physical death came to the created, and the astral world was formed, trapping souls within it. A great sorrow swept all over heaven, and an action and a pact was taken to lift fallen earthlings from their fallen state. In this action the Great White Brotherhood was formed. A Great Sisterhood was also formed.

"All of the Beings of Higher Dimensions joined forces and entered the limitations of flesh a thousand times over, to bring Light and Upliftment to a planet in despair. Many on earth today are those who thus did come also from out of our midst on these excursions of sacrifice. Many times over they have entered this alien place to bring in Light. Now we stand together in that moment upon the threshold of history, when Light shall at last rise above the darkness and a new world, and a new life will cover the earth. Rejoice beloved Ones, for your effort, and ours, have not been in vain. The earth shall rise again, and the sons of the morning shall walk in the midst, together again in the Holy Place of God's dwelling. The earth shall stand in its trial by fire, and you shall rejoice that your works have had a part in it. I AM One of the other times and Eternities."

In their Evacuation book, Lord Kuthumi had written:

"My own emanations and vibrations surround every world volunteer at this hour. I cover you with my Golden Cloak. Not one of you shall fall; not one of you shall be lost; not one of you will be touched by the Destroyer. None shall fail in your choice to complete the Mission, and not one of you shall be plucked from the Father's Hand!

ON EARTH ASSIGNMENT: THE COSMIC AWAKENING OF LIGHT WORKERS, WALK-INS AND ALL STAR-BORN REPRESENTATTIVES

"You are the Light of the World in its darkest hour. Carry on and continue the battle against that darkness. You shall be highly protected, your blessings shall be unlimited for your service to mankind."

This ground Unit of the Ashtar Command received some encouraging words from our Commander:

"You are stationed as Lights and function as Lights in dark places. Since darkness is everywhere, it matters not at this moment where your Light falls for wherever it falls it is needed. The releasing of books is as the small portions of Light from the sparkler of light, expulsed in all directions accomplishing their independent work of brightening that portion of time and space wherever they fall. Because of the prevalence of darkness, which we see as ignorance, the Light is very conspicuous in its presence. It is impossible for it to be hidden because of the very darkness it comes to remove. It is impossible for you to calculate or estimate or understand the total effect of the overall summation of light released through the work of Guardian Action International.

"What has been done will be continued on an ever-expanding scale. Do not fear to face your challenges and expansion for this is the natural function of he Light, To BE, to WORK, WHERE it is. All that is undertaken in the motivation of LOVE for the planet cannot fail in its eternal purpose. All that is done in the Name of Our Radiant One abides in a positive result forever more. Each individual soul that has been touched by your dedication has your contribution written into their record, and there are many many thousands of them. You are a supreme World Server of this hour, along with the remainder of the vast Volunteer Army of God. Not all of them have succeeded in getting or magnetizing enough energy to launch their intention. This has increased the burden for others. The magnitude of influence allotted to Guardian Action International, has taken up the loss of many who have been deterred for one reason or another in similar achievements.

"Thus it is understandable why the Brotherhood of Light has been so intent upon blessing every outreach of the energies expanded in the task of this unit. In your peculiar ministry, you do but cast your bread upon the waters, as it has been written. You know not all that is done nor who partakes of it, but all is known within the infinite records and the tiniest crumb of spiritual sustenance is never lost. This is but a moment in time compared to the eons of service that is recorded in the annals of your service to His Creation. You are not of this world, you are not of this time, you are a wanderer in the chronicles of time of the evolution of man. I AM ASHTAR of the Brotherhood of Love."

It is written that he that planteth and he that watereth are one, and every man shall receive his reward according to this labor." (1 Cor. 3:8) Thus she that writeth the books and all of they who scatter them aboard are one. All shall receive equally of the rewards of this unit. It is recorded that "They shall shine as the brightness of the firmament, and they that turn many to righteousness as the stars for ever and ever." (Dan. 12:3)

At our Anaheim Seminar in '85, a very special and select group of souls gathered, who would go on from there and do exploits for the Light. Dear Sanat Kumera knew this and He sent them this message to greet them:

"You are children of the Universe. High PRIESTS, AND KINGS. Universal Statesmen and LADIES of Great Honor from our regions. You will inexorably find your Pathway back to the Stars.

"So shall you be overshadowed, so shall you be guided and so shall you be led into your particular pathway of manifestation of the Godhead, in your world.

"You are the Special ones of the Hierarchy, who have thus lit your torch of dedication to serve the planet in its dark hour of deliverance. Therefore do the Angels overshadow you, and walk with you to sustain you.

Hierarchical Members, all of you, who have entered the Great Limitation to anchor Light upon this planet.

"I AM SANAT KUMARA who launches you into the challenge of the tasks before you." (Lord Regent of Venus)

The magnitude of the Mission is indeed overwhelming, but we abide in peace within the promise of the Beloved One, who unequivocally, and unconditionally promised His Own, "LO, I AM WITH YOU ALWAYS."

This Final Hour

The Throne Group Lords of Light, who gave us warnings earlier in this book, continue in a gentler vein:

"We bring to you greetings from the Most High, who is ready to release the forces which have been holding back these end times changes. We are encouraged by all of those who have made themselves ready for this final episode. There is nothing to fear. It is truly going to be a glorious time for those who know how it all ends. We are certain you will be pleased to know that the Light Forces will not have to go through all of the agony of the Apocalypse. This has been averted by those who have come in the Name of the Father to serve here on planet Earth. They have accomplished a wonderful work in turning the tide of disaster. We welcome home all of those who are ready to return after the mission is completed. This is a time of great rejoicing for all who have given so much in the Name of the Father.

"Now that the fallen ones have been removed from the Higher Realms, the Light is shining brightly upon the planet. There will be much confusion in lower realms now that the fallen ones are there. They will create much chaos in the immediate future, for they will have no place to go. This is a time to retain all of your energies for the final battle. This battle involves all of the forces of darkness including those who have returned to this arena of war against the Light. They of course will fail, but we must let them have their day.

"Most of the Light Forces upon the planet will be receiving parts of these dictations through their subconscious. There is a wide broadcast being made to alert our workers that all has been brought into harmony in the Higher Realms; nor is there anything to fear in terms of unseen influences. What will appear as total chaos to those who are not aware of the plan, will simply be a final closing to this dramatic chapter in Universal History. That which has been happening in the Higher Realms has been far more spectacular in terms of total energy expended, than what is about to happen in the Earth plane.

"We realize this may be little consolation for those who must still complete their mission, but it is certainly a relief to those who understand the magnitude of what has just been completed. We have all been waiting in great anticipation for these end days for a very long time. You must remember that many of you have been fighting the battle in many different planes and this has been very trying on your souls and etheric bodies. We welcome this relief for all of those who have gone through this process."

ON EARTH ASSIGNMENT: THE COSMIC AWAKENING OF LIGHT WORKERS, WALK-INS AND ALL STAR-BORN REPRESENTATTIVES

I am recalling the account of 80 United States soldiers from Fort Dix who had become trapped by flames while fighting a nearby forest fire. They were unaware the fire had almost completely surrounded them and continued vigorously to fight on. Overhead an aircraft, having perceived the predicament, flew low at great risk and dropped weighted notes. This was repeated three times before the soldiers saw and retrieved the messages. The message explained their situation and the fact that now only one narrow flame-lined channel remained through which he could lead them if they would follow. Those soldiers were not fools! They dropped their equipment and ran along the narrow strip to follow the craft leading them; a strip bordered by roaring flames. They all reached safety, thanks to their belief in the message and the higher guidance which could see the whole scene. If they had stopped to argue and debate the truthfulness of the message there would have been 80 charred, blackened bodies on the bleak, barren New Jersey countryside. But instead they believed the only ones whose position above could see the entire situation.

The Beloved Lords of Light from the Highest Celestia project one last message your way:

"We are the Lords of Light, a group whose deepest concern is with all of you and your collective welfare on all levels of Being. I AM Michael, with Jesus Sananda, Beloved Mary, Kuthumi and Ashtar, all who join with me in this our final statement to conclude this written effort to be released to this generation.

"We have reviewed these messages, the teachings that are included in this work of our chosen messenger, who has so conscientiously given all her energies, her time, her talents, to place before you our words and our warnings to see you through that which is in your pathway at this time. We commend her efforts and we urge you most sincerely to give your attention to the word herein compiled.

"We have been sounding a trumpet call in a lethargic world, one which can scarcely give such things a moment of their time. Nevertheless, that moment in time now comes when all else must be laid aside and the attention be drawn to the things of the Soul. The Heart must now be fixed in Love upon the Heavenly Father, the Creator, in whose hands all things are held in abeyance until that moment when the true trials of mankind will be upon him.

"We have sent our words, we have sent our warnings. All humanity must pause and give thought to the path that lies before you. Thoughts and intent must be brought into focus with the Divine Plan for this planet.

"The harvest of many lifetimes is about to take place for every Soul. The corruption that abounds in your world will soon be removed by many means. The degradation of man will be tolerated no longer by the Entity that is this planet. She shall shake herself, and rid herself of that which defiles her purity and her purpose. The manifestation of her wrath will wash away every impurity from her, and bring about a new creation of cleanliness and beauty.

"The sands of time have slowly sifted their granules until the hourglass Now has emptied itself. That moment is here when the Angel shall stand with one foot upon the land and one upon the sea and declare 'THERE SHALL BE TIME NO LONGER.'

"We are the Lords of Light, from the Great Central Sun of energies abundant for this planet who has served mankind so faithfully. We stand now to surround her with our Angels of the Apocalypse. We support her in her hour of retribution. None shall blaspheme her bounty anymore. She has reached the fullness of her fury against those who would destroy her purpose and her plan. Now is the time she must express within her innermost being that which is her destiny. We of the Most High can no longer suppress or deny her this right of expression, our hand is removed from her that she shall be given her final hour of retribution.

"Mankind now stands ready to absorb truth and the lessons before him. In this final hour many thousands shall return to the Father in their new found awareness of the spiritual options that yet remain. We have listed events as they must come and the lessons they embrace.

"Those who have waited so long for this day shall wait no longer. Those who have labored so faithfully through the centuries shall rest from their labors. Those who have plotted the darkness shall stand no longer when the fountains of the great deep shall speak. Behold the Father shall create a new dimension of beauty, harmony and Love forevermore. The Earth shall know her reward and shall come to her day of destiny in the

ON EARTH ASSIGNMENT: THE COSMIC AWAKENING OF LIGHT WORKERS, WALK-INS AND ALL STAR-BORN REPRESENTATTIVES

fullness of Divine Purpose to all of the Cosmos."

Lord Hatton speaks:

"Nature will follow its course in its reaction to that which man has done to it. It can respond in no other way. Therefore, it was inevitable that those who must serve from the ground level had to be prepared and trained, briefed, and told in detail that which is to come. We have softened the message in every way possible to avoid panic or fear for mankind, but we speak to you who are a part of us that these things must come to pass. The planet will~ in time, be totally recovered and be entirely new.

"At this point in time, there are Souls who want the details of their purpose and mission. The best that we can do is to lift you into our presence and give you individually, one by one, interviews and opportunities to discuss every phase of the future with you. This we have done and propose to continue to do. Be not carried away by the rosy messages of those who would say that nothing of consequence shall take place on this planet. It is indeed quite contrary from every level of approach to planetary life. Change must come.

"Our part is merely to do our very best with all of the knowledge, technology and equipment that we have to assist mankind when these things come, and to rescue and protect our own, whom we have sent.

"There will be a remaining with us, until the planet is indeed new again. When it is a new Earth, then life shall go on, on a higher level of evolution, in fellowship, in all of the ways you so desire now, for which you are so eager; but they are coming. That day is coming. We are one with you, and you are one with us. We are your Brothers and Sisters of the Ashtar Command, and I AM Hatton."

Innkeepers of the Galaxy

Late this spring, I was deeply impressed by a channeled message from Ashtar, received from messenger Tuieta (Portals of Light) at Fort Wayne, Indiana. The message was geared to center the attention of mankind once again, upon the seriousness of the planetary situation.

"How many times must this be brought to your attention? Even

ON EARTH ASSIGNMENT: THE COSMIC AWAKENING OF
LIGHT WORKERS, WALK-INS AND ALL STAR-BORN REPRESENTATTIVES

the forces of Light dawdle in preparation. Many have great difficulty with the commitment made before embodiment!

"Leaders of government can you not see the pain, the suffering, the needless slaughter that is taking place merely by the stroke of your pens, the wave of your hands? Can you not feel the sacredness of that which is the breath of Life?

"There are those who would seek to discredit us (The Ashtar Command) and that which we would share. They can accomplish nothing except that which the workers of Light would ALLOW THEM TO ACCOMPLISH. We are HERE. We are not the figment of one's imagination. We do not choose to manifest merely to satisfy the curiosity of the ill prepared and ill-informed. We are on a mission of mercy in the name of the Divine Creator. We have no need to digress TO THE CHILDISH GAMES that ones would put forth to satisfy their own egos. Be advised this hour that all stabilization has been removed from the belt of Earth. Be advised this hour that intercessory measures shall be taken by our Fleets only in the following circumstances:

"-when worldly activities are such that they would have an adverse impact upon the Universe and total cosmos;

"-when Earth activities indicate that there is the probability of destroying the planet creating Cosmic effect;

"-when Earth volunteers from distant realms and galaxies are in immediate danger, we would intercede immediately;

"-when there is a dominance of negative polarization at the expense of the totality of the inhabitants, which is denied by the Cosmic Law.

"In any of these instances we would by Cosmic Law have right of intercession."

This represents one of the most important message received from the Commander ' for the entire year. Not only because it addresses the closed-minded nitpickers who criticize that which they do not understand, but also because here we are given a concise guideline of those eventualities which would cancel out the Universal edict of non-interference in Cosmic affairs. We salute Tuieta for this fine work.

Make no mistake about it. The Inns of Heaven are ready, awaiting their guests. Nothing is crowded in these self-contained phenomenally organized, incredibly spacious, floating etheric worlds. Seven of these great Pearly White Space Cities are said to be in readiness, which vary in size from 100 miles in diameter to the largest of all, which houses the headquarters of Lord Jesus Sananda, Lord Ashtar and the Ashtar Command. It is said to be over 100 miles in diameter.

The Great Space Cities have 12 levels (in most cases) and it has occurred to me that you would enjoy a tour to inspect one of them.

Approaching, we first see underneath level one, which is the great entry and exit portal for trafficking craft. It consists of disembarking platforms, parking docks, garages for incoming visiting craft, maintenance departments, and storage areas for the thousands of small scout ships cleverly stacked like so many Oreo cookies. An interesting facility here is Registration Headquarters. In this area all incoming personages must register their presence with the great computer system, as well as register their departure. (Have you ever had so much company in your house that you didn't know where they all were at any given time?) No one will get lost or overlooked on this glorious craft.

The second level might be termed a colossal stockroom. This is the Quartermaster Deck, containing all manner of supplies and inventories for the varied needs of all levels. It is like a city of warehouses, but immaculately clean of course.

The third level is a vast zoo. It is the level set aside for animal husbandry research, and birdland. Every manner of creature from many worlds has a habitat here. It is rather a noisy level, but the air there is nevertheless pure and pleasant.

Above it, level four is designated for Agricultural research. It is like a vast farmland of well kept vegetable and botanical garden fruit orchards and sample specimens brought on board from various worlds for reseeding on new worlds and activity of that nature. Much of the growth is blue instead of green.

ON EARTH ASSIGNMENT: THE COSMIC AWAKENING OF
LIGHT WORKERS, WALK-INS AND ALL STAR-BORN REPRESENTATTIVES

The fifth level is a housing center for all those technicians and persons who serve on the four levels beneath.

Directly above five, is the breathtakingly beautiful recreational level and lushly landscaped park areas, where a relaxing stroll is a sheer joy. All manner of recreational activities are located here for access by all residents of all ages.

Strategically located, level seven is the sprawling Medical Complex. Awesome in size, many information centers are needed to guide one. It contains all comprehensive patient facilities and quarters for all medical personnel. Dental care areas, biological research centers, and the ship's laboratories; all elaborated with the finest technology Space has to offer.

The eighth level is the housing prepared for Earth's evacuees. It contains staterooms for individuals and apartments for families as far as one can see. These areas are dotted with countless joint dining areas, social halls, nursery care sections, laundry facilities and of course information offices. Gradually ship guests are introduced to the technologies of these various areas, an exciting experience.

Level nine is their prized University Compound. The Halls of Wisdom, vast libraries scattered everywhere, endless concert halls and cultural interests from throughout the Galaxy. Halls of learning house classes with curricula for all ages. Very young children's classrooms are filled with individualized computer systems. Rooms are decorated with domed ceilings colorful in their display of planets and words as they progress across the pathless sky, each at a different pace. Elementary astronomy is taught to the very young and they quickly learn to identify and name the various planets and sections of the universe. Vibrant vitality shines in their faces as they have conversations with their computers.

Musical talent blossoms in outer space because of the music rooms in the great craft. There one can play upon an instrument, in a soundproof room, along with a full orchestration background on a wide choice of selections by merely pressing the correct buttons on a computer panel. Any category of music, with hundreds of selections, are available at the fingertips of the lone but aspiring soloist.

**ON EARTH ASSIGNMENT: THE COSMIC AWAKENING OF
LIGHT WORKERS, WALK-INS AND ALL STAR-BORN REPRESENTATTIVES**

On level ten, these innkeepers of the galaxy house their visiting dignitaries from all dimensions, in special apartments. This tenth level is also primarily barracks for the EX's, staterooms and apartments with multiple scattered conference rooms and beautiful sprawling dining and lounge areas.

The home for the ASHTAR COMMAND HEADQUARTERS is located on level eleven, also the Great Rotunda Meeting Hall. Summoned by a soft electronic tone in their quarters, Earth evacuees are brought to this Great Hall for any necessary group gatherings. Its striking circular wall displays many tremendous viewing screens, where guests are permitted to view Cosmic panorama as well as their own world and things to come as well as things passed. The Great Hall is also used for auspicious social occasions, like welcoming and meeting with visiting dignitaries or other festivities from any level. This level also houses the viewing room, map room, and Soul-Panel boards, which was once Athena's domain; and finally the enormous Command Communications Center, where all Earth contacts are precipitated or monitored, recorded, or whatever, as well as inter Command communication.

Level twelve is the uppermost portion of the craft and is referred to as "THE DOME." It is the officer's Observation Desk and pilot control center. Earth visitors are permitted here in groups, by appointment. The total surrounding circumference is furnished with comfortable chairs for relaxing and observation. Rap sessions with crew members are a part of the experience there.

The defense system of the Mother Craft is housed in the lowest and this highest level, as well as at the outermost edge of the other individual levels, across from the circle roadways. These defense systems are not in evidence, but can be activated on a moment's notice, in conjunction with the tremendous communications system throughout the entire Command. These defense systems, of course, do not see any action in this time of galactic events.

Directly down through the center of the great ship, all levels share a circular shaft or center core which is a power reactor throughout the craft. However, one must remember that the activating source of power comes from the Universe itself; this is but its channel to proper sources. The power center core is roughly 200 feet or so in diameter. (I'm not good at that distinction.) Its outer shell contains several primary elevators (or large lifts) for inter-level transportation. A few larger lifts are restricted for Quartermaster and maintenance use. At each level, the power center is surrounded by a spacious lounging area, beautifully furnished and shared by all divisions of that level.

Generally speaking, the ship's furnishings are simple and sharp in design. White is the predominant color, contrasted with stirring tones of orange or reds or blues, and much yellow. The colors are all pure, not muddied or muted. In earth terms, the decor would be described as ultra modern, with its gleaming use of a glasslike substance similar to our Lucite accessories.

Transportation is interesting. The perimeter of each level is circumvented with a roadway which is used to arrive at different areas or sections of the level, not unlike the traffic beltways that surrounded earth cities. Parks~ all along this outer roadway (at each level) are unending lines of little transporting vehicles accessible for all to use, somewhat reminiscent of earth motorcycles with sidecars, but these are of course silent in their maneuvering. (Talk about heaven!) From the center core lounges to the outer core roadway, there are four other major connective roadways, which symbolically combine with the lower panel circle to form the four nodes of the Solar Cross Symbol, as one looks downward upon it (see diagram below).

Two lesser routes divide each quadrant identified as number one through twelve. Thus locating anything is totally simple, being identified as 12/4, which would represent level twelve and section four; 8/6 would be level eight, the sixth section and so on.

Friends, when you see the sky blackened with thousands of small craft coming in to carry you to these great cities, be not afraid. See, instead, the end to all the tears you have shed; those tears of despair which came from a heart grieving for a gentler time; a safe haven from a world of harshness. These ships mean our deliverance! They mean that the time of love and beauty you have prayed for has arrived! So reach out your hand in gratitude to your loving Father because he has indeed "many mansions," prepared and waiting for you from the foundation of the world.

ON EARTH ASSIGNMENT: THE COSMIC AWAKENING OF LIGHT WORKERS, WALK-INS AND ALL STAR-BORN REPRESENTATTIVES

Soon comes the day, when we ascend
Waving Love to Earth, our dear Friend
All doubt forever ... in the past
Death's shadow now ... no longer cast
Hear the words, of our Father, from out, the Great Sun,
"Welcome Home, my child... well done, well done."
Behold the Tabernacle of God is With Men

I am told by our Extraterrestrial friends that it will take at least seven years for planet Earth to heal over the scars of her tribulation. Panoramic pastures of flowers and lush greenery will be set aside to replenish in beauty, spots where polluted cities once stood and wars were fought. These will not be touched for centuries, but left to blossom until all scars are completely healed deep beneath them.

The many combined fleets of the ASHTAR COMMAND will be occupied balancing the magnetic grid system to restore it to positive and accurate balance once again. Evacuees from Earth will observe this from viewing screens on the great Mother craft, as space ships beyond number of all colors, tints, shapes, sizes, some just as balls of radiant Light, travel at incredible speeds along every line of the grid system, moving in beautiful precision.

They will anchor the Earth within its own forcefield and reopen the planetary chakras where new beautiful cities will be built. They will also clear the dimensional portals for the later entry of the immense, city-sized ships, which will return their precious cargo to the planet. This will come after Earth's glorious restoration when all things will be made new.

"The people that walked in darkness have seen a great Light; they that dwelt in the land of the shadow of death, upon them hath the Light shined. For unto us a Child is born, unto us a Son is given; and the Government shall be upon His Shoulders; and His name shall be called Wonderful, Counselor, The Mighty God, the Everlasting Father, The Prince of Peace. Every valley shall be exalted, and every mountain and hill shall be made low; and the crooked shall be made straight, and the rough places plain. They that wait upon the Lord shall renew their strength; they shall mount up with wings as Eagles; they shall run and not weary, and shall walk and not faint.

ON EARTH ASSIGNMENT: THE COSMIC AWAKENING OF LIGHT WORKERS, WALK-INS AND ALL STAR-BORN REPRESENTATTIVES

"I have called thee by thy name, thou art mine. When you passeth though the waters, I will be with thee; and through the rivers, they - shall not overflow thee; when THOU WALKEST THROUGH THE FIRE, thou shall not be burned; neither shall the flame kindle upon thee.

"Then shall thy Light break forth as the morning, and thine health shall spring forth speedily; and thy righteousness shall go before thee; the glory of the Lord shall be thy reward. Then shalt thou call, and the Lord shall answer; thou shalt cry, and he shall say, Here I AM. And the Lord shall guide thee continually, and satisfy thy soul in drought, and thou shalt be like a watered garden, like a spring of waters whose waters fail not. And they that be of thee, shall build the old waste places; thou shalt raise up the foundations of many generations; and thou shalt be called the repairer of the breach, THE RESTORER OF PATHS TO DWELL IN." (Isa. 9:2,6, 40:4,31, 43:1,2, 58:8-12)

Commander Lord Ashtar once described Shan Chea as the largest of the Father's great orbiting cities that encircle this Solar System and primarily this planet. It orbits from 500 to 1500 miles away from Earth, varying this height from time to time. It remains fixed in certain holding patterns when circumstances require it. It is one of the slower moving bodies because of its size and because of its monitoring of the overall area as well as its monitoring of Earth's inhabitants. It has been in orbit since long before the coming of the Christ Child. Its orbit is not given to any certain pathway, for it goes wherever it is led by needs and situations. It is the Great White City upon which Our Beloved Commander abides most of the time, and from which He projects all of His Energies to the system. Many times it hovers at the portal of this Universe when great Inter Universal Councils take place.

Earlier in this manuscript, I briefly touched upon an experience where it had been my privilege to visit with Commander Soltec on his craft, the Phoenix, during an out-of-body excursion. Because it was to be reported to the Light workers through Universal Network, a full recall had been permitted.

On the ship, I was courteously seated before three very large viewing screens in his office and laboratory rotunda. The center screen presented a sweeping panorama of Earth's landscape; beautiful snow scenes, then tropical areas, majestic green mountains, colorful oceans, like

ON EARTH ASSIGNMENT: THE COSMIC AWAKENING OF
LIGHT WORKERS, WALK-INS AND ALL STAR-BORN REPRESENTATTIVES

a travelogue on a tremendous scale and utterly beautiful. It seemed somewhat strange to me that in this broad viewing I saw no housing of any description or any evidence of commercial or city life; in fact I saw no human life at all. Soltec was evidently reading my thoughts. He commented:

"You are now viewing the planet as it will be when it is cleansed and new in its glory and beauty; just before that time when it is populated again. This is the new growth, the new covering that will bloom upon the planet when the people of Light set foot upon it. Notice how much more beautiful is the greenery of the vegetation and the spreading trees, the deep blue of the firmament, the clear cleanliness of the water, for all pollution and deterrents are now removed from the atmosphere. The air is pure and clean."

He zoomed in on a tremendous pasture of wild flowers. The colorful splash was breathtaking. He smiled and told me, "On that very panorama a large polluting dirty city formally stood." I would never have recognized the terrain, though I had once lived in that city. He further stated, "Many spots on the beautiful Earth that have suffered degradation at the hands of mankind, will be left to rest."

The screen to the left was activated and revealed a desirable landscape of sloping hills lavishly covered with trees of that heavenly (!) green, many beautiful broad open areas in its midst. There were creeks, and slow flowing rivers. I could see the rocks at the bottom through the clear water, even from our distant vantage point.

Suddenly high above these vast central planes I saw the gleaming bright light of a Spacecraft, very brilliant, glowing as it lowered and settled down silently, gently on the miles of greenery. It was a beautiful ship of indescribable size. I can only say it was extremely spacious, shiningly beautiful, dominating the screen as we watched, and my heart pounded fiercely.

Many openings suddenly appeared all around the vast city, with wide stairways dropping down, efficiently and quickly. Upon each one, crowds of people; youth, tots, perched on adult shoulders or clutching the hands of parents while hugging all of their young pets the Space friends had given them. All begin to descend at once in a run, screaming with joy or in prayer, but happiness and smiles everywhere. The high emotion of

ON EARTH ASSIGNMENT: THE COSMIC AWAKENING OF
LIGHT WORKERS, WALK-INS AND ALL STAR-BORN REPRESENTATTIVES

the moment was contagious and I found myself feeling exhilarated along with them and smiling broadly as well. I looked at the Commander, and he also was smiling and laughing with great joy.

"What's happening here, sir?"

"This is the first landing of persons and Light workers returning to the new Earth."

I caught my breath as I marveled at their happiness. As far as you could see, they were running all over the beautiful hills and the young children were very occupied with sharing pets and pats on their little creatures. These were all children born in outer space on the great craft; what a heritage they had, facing a new life that would share fellowship with these beautiful souls from other worlds. There were many infants also, carried as the throng continued to pour from the opening and down the many stairways. They streamed forth by the hundreds, until finally I calculated there must be several thousands disembarking.

My gazed fixed upon one young woman seated on the grass, who had picked a colorful bouquet, clutching it to her bosom and weeping tears of happiness all over the blossoms. She had a kitten who romped playfully beside her.

At a few of the exits, the Space Friends widen the doorways in some manner, and expose tremendous cages filled with birds of every imaginable specie. As the sides of the cages were lifted, the creatures escaped forth with a great hum from the sound of their wings; shadowing the sun as this living cloud swept out and onward into the new land. The crowds pointed skyward as they watched the ascent.

Coming our way from around the ship, a long, continuous string of the little vehicles that had lined the craft roadways, were now brought out for access. After a considerable passing of time, the stream of humanity ceased from filing down the stairways. Then the Space Brothers began to follow the procession. At each exit hundreds of them in their shiny suits carried much equipment. Each was heavy laden with various boxes or packages and armloads of assorted gear, as the crowd gathered around them expectantly.

ON EARTH ASSIGNMENT: THE COSMIC AWAKENING OF
LIGHT WORKERS, WALK-INS AND ALL STAR-BORN REPRESENTATTIVES

Then a roar from the crowd as the animals gingerly started their procession down the planks. There descended a parade of young animals, a beautiful fawn stepped proudly upon the grassy knolls, clusters of squirrels and chipmunks jumped off the planks scurrying into the deeper grass. To the joy of the children, lambs pounced on the scene. Many young kids for future milk goats bound for the ground, followed by many sprinting, kicking, lively young colts.

Finally the moment came when the activity had stilled and a hush of reverence swept across the masses. Every eye was turned toward the massive center portal which seemed to glow in an invisible Light. Suddenly three beautiful Beings appeared atop the stairs and paused. As I sat with Soltec viewing the scene, intuitively, I knew they were Lord Jesus Sananda, Lord Kuthumi, and Lord Saint Germain. The shorter of the three was draped in a violet colored cape. Lord Jesus wore a simple white robe girded at the center, and Lord Kuthumi was clothed in a golden colored metallic appearing robe. Together, they descended where the assembled stood waiting. They clasped as many outstretched hands as possible and embraced many. I realized these Beloved Ones and the Space Friends would be remaining with them for considerable time.

As the screen projections were about to conclude, my vision traced the descent of many other craft, smaller, sweeping in to land at distant spots. Soltec identified them as being technicians and builders, coming to help these happy pioneers build their homes and necessary structures to begin their life on the New Earth.

The three Light Beings, returning to the huge ship, turned to face the crowd again at the portal, where Lord Jesus raised His Hands in blessing, smiling gently, in His benediction upon the new world citizenry ... the Father's flock!

We thank our friend Soltec for sharing these beautiful details with all of us. We close this effort on your behalf, on this loving note of blessed hope within our Beings, for that great and glorious day when Earth shall be new and these things shall come to pass. Even so ... Lord Jesus ... come QUICKLY!

ON EARTH ASSIGNMENT: THE COSMIC AWAKENING OF LIGHT WORKERS, WALK-INS AND ALL STAR-BORN REPRESENTATTIVES

"And I saw a new Earth and I, John, saw the Holy City, New Jerusalem, coming down from God out of Heaven and I heard a great Voice out of Heaven saying, Behold, the tabernacle of God is with men, and He will dwell with them and they shall be His people, and God Himself shall be with them, and He their God shall wipe away all tears from their eyes; for the former things are passed away, Behold, I make all things new. He carried me away in the spirit to a great and High Mountain, and showed me that great City descending out of Heaven from God." (Rev. 21)

"Behold, I create New Heavens, and a New Earth; and the former shall not be remembered, nor come into mind."

"They shall build houses and inhabit them and they shall plant vineyards and eat the fruit of them. They shall not build and another inhabit; they shall not plant and another eat; for as the days of a tree are the days of my people, and mine Elect shall long enjoy the work of -their hands. For they are the seed of the Blessed of the Lord, and their offspring with them."

"Before they call, I will answer; and while they are yet speaking, I will hear. The wolf and the lamb shall feed together, and the lion shall eat straw like the bullock, they shall not hurt nor destroy in all my Holy Mountata. They shall beat their swords into plowshares; neither shall they Learn War Anymore." Isaiah 65:17-25,2:4.

About The Author-Tuella

Tuella's "calling" as a *Messenger of Light* began in the early seventies with her channeling work commissioned personally by Ashtar on behalf of the Intergalactic Space Confederation. In addition to *Project World Evacuation*, her future works to be published by Inner Light include *Messengers For The Coming Decade, Ashtar: A Tribute, On Earth Assignment,* and *The Dynamics of Cosmic Telepathy.*

EXPLORE THE PAST, PRESENT AND FUTURE

ANCIENT ASTRONAUTS AND GEORGE HUNT WILLIAMSON

LEGACY OF THE SKY PEOPLE: *The Extraterrestrial Origin of Adam and Eve; The Garden of Eden; Noah's Ark and the Serpent Race* by Brinsley Le Poer Trench (8th Earl of Clancarty) with Nick Redfern—*Proof of ancient astronauts could cause worldwide religious, political and energy upheavals!* As early as the 1960s, Britain's 8th Earl of Clancarty, Brinsley Le Poer Trench, made an astounding revelation. He was convinced that life on earth originated on the planet Mars and that the first voyagers here had been the Biblical Adam and Eve who had left their paradise of the Garden of Eden and arrived on earth in a space ark piloted by Noah. Thus the roots of the various Biblical stories from the Old Testament which are taught in every Sunday School today.
8.5" x 11"—228 pages—ISBN-13: 978-1606111277—$21.95

ALIEN SPACE GODS OF ANCIENT GREECE AND ROME BY W.R. DRAKE—*Was the Mediterranean Region of our planet visited by a race of "super Beings" in ancient times? Was the Oracle of Delphi a conduit for prophetic messages from outer space?*—Questions Answered. . . Did giants from space establish a UFO base atop the picturesque Mount Olympus? Were they the gods and goddesses of "Mythology" idolized and given names such as Apollo, Hades, Athena, Hermes, Zeus, Artemis and Hestia? Did the powerful deities of Greece help save Athens from being invaded by the mighty armies of Atlantis in 10,000 BC? Were omens observed in the sky just before the murder of Caesar?
7X9"—318 pages— ISBN-13: 9781606110973—$21.95

ANCIENT SECRETS OF MYSTERIOUS AMERICA: REVEALING OUR TRUE COSMIC DESTINY BY W.R. DRAKE, WITH JOSHUA SHAPIRO—*Do strange alien artifacts discovered throughout the Americas prove ancient astronauts once winged to Earth and shared their wisdom with early humans?*—Did the Gods mate with virgins to father heroes whose wondrous deeds inspired their people to new glories? Tradition tells of shadowy figures, not born of woman, flitting down the dusty corridors of time to preach some new philosophy or invent some novel machine, thus revolutionizing contemporary culture.
8.5x11"—190 pages—ISBN-13: 978-1606111024—$15.95

TRAVELING THE PATH BACK TO THE ROAD IN THE SKY by George Hunt Williamson with Nick Redfern and Brad Steiger—*A strange saga of saucers, space brothers and secret agents.* Within these pages are the stories of the Hopi Sun Clan, including the legends of the "Giant Star." Stone Tablets of Peru. The Time Spanners. The Beacon of the Gods. Martian Miniatures. Fossils, Footprints and Fantasy. Evidence for the existence of the "Silent World," reality of the Unholy Six. The strange disappearance of his friends Hunrath and Wilkinson – were they abducted by aliens in 1955?
8.5x11"—300 pages—ISBN-13: 978-1606111338—$24.00

Mail Order customers order by title, please.

THE SAUCERS SPEAK: CALLING ALL OCCUPANTS OF INTERPLANETARY CRAFT by George Hunt Williamson with Sean Castel and Tim Beckley—It is not necessary to construct giant interstellar telecommunication dishes to send amateurish binary signals out into the universe. There is intelligent life in the Universe and we have already communicated with beings on other worlds!
8.5x11"—136 pages
ISBN-13: 978-1606111321—$15.95

OTHER TONGUES, OTHER FLESH REVISITED by George Hunt Williamson—*Ancient mysteries collide with today's cosmic realities.* There are many types of visitors coming to earth. They come in many disguises. . . Most are friendly. A few are NOT! They include: THE WANDERERS – THE MIGRANTS – THE PROPHETS —THE HARVESTERS – THE AGENTS – THE INTRUDERS – THE GUESSERS. Here are SECRETS concerning the creation of life and the evolution of humankind entrusted to only a handful.
8.5x11"—214 pages —$24.00
ISBN-13: 978-1606110522

ASHTAR COMMAND AND CHANNELED TITLES

PROJECT WORLD EVACUATION by the Ashtar Command as channeled by Tuella—UFOs To Assist In The "Great Exodus" Of Human Souls Off This Planet. Friendly ETs to save the "chosen" during a forthcoming great global disaster. New Age "rapture."
8.5x11"—134 pages —
ISBN-13: 978-0938294375—$18.95

A NEW BOOK OF REVELATIONS by the Ashtar Command as channeled by Tuella—*A Harvesting Of Souls At Earth's Final Moment - A Grand Deception For The "Last Days."*—Here are shocking revelations from the highest spiritual powers in the Universe that will balance your chakras and tune-up your soul.
8.5x11"—146 pages—ISBN-13: 978-0938294856—$18.95

ASHTAR: REVEALING THE SECRETS OF THE FORCES OF LIGHT by Tuella—*Man or Myth? Name or Title? Space Commander or Archangel? Intergalactic Spiritual Leader?* —The name Ashtar has become widely known in UFO Channeling circles for several decades. It is said that his messages are being beamed from a colossal Starship — or Space Station — beyond our atmosphere.
8.5x11"—142 pages—ISBN-13: 978-0938294290—$18.95

THE LAST BOOKS of Tuella
With Material From The Ashtar Command:
Master Symbol of the Solar Cross & A New Book of Revelations

HERE ARE THE SECRET MASTER KEYS TO THE GREAT AWAKENING. . . FOR THE FIRST TIME THE SPIRITUAL HIERARCHY EXPOSES THE UNIVERSAL LAWS OF . . LIFE – MAGNETIC RESONANCE – ACTION AND REACTION – LIGHT — VIBRATION – MIND – HARMONY – DIMENSIONS – LOVE – POLARITY – ATTRACTION – MANIFESTATION

Following the death of the well respected channel Tuella – primary representative for the Ashtar Command on Earth – her important last manuscript, ***THE MASTER SYMBOL OF THE SOLAR CROSS*** became impossible to obtain. This work contains the key symbols that offer us the basic laws governing every phase of our awareness as a complete unit of being. Here are the Universal Laws that can make us co-creative spirits of God. Here is the Great Awakening that will enable us to evolve toward a consciousness of the basic oneness of all life. This is the Great Lesson of absolute necessity of our living in accordance with the Laws of Creation. OVER 300 LARGE SIZE PAGES, THIS WORK COMES WITH AN ACTUAL CHANNELING SESSION – CONVERTED TO AUDIO CD – as given by the space entity known as Monka, as well as the only recorded lecture give by Tuella known to exist. ***MASTER SYMBOL OF THE SOLAR CROSS*** was $50.00 – now just $29.95

Also Newly Revised: A NEW BOOK OF REVELATIONS —
A HARVESTING OF SOULS AT EARTH'S FINAL MOMENT: A GRAND DECEPTION FOR THE "LAST DAYS"

You are about the participate in the most fabulous transformation of humankind ever experienced. Here are shocking revelations from the highest spiritual powers in the universe that will balance your chakras and tune-up your soul. These are the final messages and warnings from the Ashtar Command, the Space Brotherhood, and the Masters of Universal Wisdom. This work corrects many of the misconceptions and inaccurate translations made of the Old and New Testaments and lays the foundation for *"A New Book of Revelations"* as transcribed to Tuella, the official representative for outer space and inner consciousness. Now is the time to get ready for the ***GREAT CHANGES*** to happen in our lifetime!

Order ***A NEW BOOK OF REVELATIONS*** for just $20.00

Both Titles $44.00 + $5.00 S/H

**SUPER SPECIAL
ALL ITEMS THIS PAGE
JUST $99.00 + $8.00 S/H**

Two Books Above And These Four Books

OTHER ASHTAR COMMAND BOOKS AVAILABLE
☐ PROJECT WORLD EVACUATION - $20.00
☐ ASHTAR REVEALING HIS SECRET IDENTITY - $20.00
☐ ON EARTH ASSIGNMENT - $20.00
☐ THE SPACE PEOPLE SPEAK - $14.00

Timothy Beckley, Box 753, New Brunswick, NJ 08903
24/7 credit card answering machine: 732 602-3407 - PayPal Orders MrUFO8@hotmail.com

ON EARTH ASSIGNMENT: THE COSMIC AWAKENING OF LIGHT WORKERS, WALK-INS AND ALL STAR-BORN REPRESENTATTIVES